PREVENTING VIOLENCE IN THE WORKPLACE

We gratefully acknowledge the following:

"The Accuracy of Predictions of Violence to Others," by C. Lidz et al., *Journal of American Medical Associations*, February 24, 1993. Reprinted with permission.

"Best Practices in White-Collar Downsizing: Managing Contradictions," by K. S. Cameron et al., *Academy of Management Executive*, August 1991, pp. 57–73.

"Cease Fire! Preventing Workplace Violence," by Bob Smith, *HR FOCUS*, February 1994. Copyright 1994, American Management Association, New York. All rights reserved.

Corporate Culture and Performance, by John P. Kotter and James L. Heskett. Copyright 1992 by Kotter Associates, Inc., and James L. Heskett. Adapted with the permission of The Free Press, a Division of Simon & Schuster, Inc.

"Dangerous and Violent Behavior," by John Monahan, Ph.D., *Journal of Occupational Medicine*, October-December 1986. Reprinted with permission.

"Dodging the Bullet," by Eric Raimy. Reprinted with permission of *Human Resource Executive*. Copyright 1993. All rights reserved. For subscription information, call 215-784-0860.

"Downsizing: What Do We Know? What Have We Learned?" by Wayne F. Cascio, University of Colorado, *Academy of Management Executive*, February 1993, pp. 95–104.

Fear and Violence in the Workplace, 1993, Northwestern National Life Insurance Company.

"Guidance on Giving Counsel," by Paula Lynn Parks, *Los Angeles Times*, July 11, 1994.

"Let the Good Times Roll—And a Few More Heads." Reprinted from January 31, 1994, issue of *Business Week* by special permission, copyright 1994 by McGraw-Hill, Inc.

"Limiting Therapist Exposure to Tarasoff Liability: Guidelines for Risk Containment," by John Monahan, Ph.D., *American Psychologist*, March 1993. Copyright 1993, The American Psychological Association. Adapted by permission.

"Mental Disorder and Violent Behavior: Perceptions and Evidence," by John Monahan, Ph.D., *American Psychologist*, April 1992. Copyright 1992, The American Psychological Association. Adapted by permission.

On Death and Dying, by Elisabeth Kübler-Ross, Simon & Schuster, Inc. Copyright 1969 by Elisabeth Kübler-Ross, M.D.

"Prosecutors Taking Harder Line Toward Spouse Abuse," by Bettina Boxall and Frederick M. Muir, *Los Angeles Times*, July 11, 1994. Copyright *Los Angeles Times*. Reprinted by permission.

Prosser and Keaton on the Law of Torts, 5th ed., 1984. With permission of West Publishing Corporation.

"Safe and Sound: Caseworker Safety in the Delivery of Social Service," by J. Irwin, unpublished (New York: Institute for Families and Children).

"Violence in the Workplace," by John Monahan, Ph.D. *Journal of Occupational Medicine*, October 1990. Reprinted with permission.

"When Employees Kill Other Employees: The Case of Joseph T. Wesbecker," by Frank Kuzmits, Ph.D., *Journal of Occupational Medicine*, October 1990. Reprinted with permission.

"When Violence Hits Business," by Linda Thornburg, *HR Magazine*, July 1993.

"Witnesses Tell of Shooting at Convair Plant," by Mark Platte, *Los Angeles Times*, March 14, 1992. Copyright *Los Angeles Times*. Reprinted by permission.

"Workplace Time Bombs Can Be Diffused," by Gerald T. Brandt and Joseph M. Brennan. Reprinted with permission of *Human Resource Professional*. Copyright 1993 by LRP Publications, 747 Dresher Road, P.O. Box 980, Horsham, PA 19044-0980. All rights reserved. For more information on *Human Resource Professional* or other human resource products published by LRP Publications, please call 800-341-7874, ext. 246.

"Workplace Violence: Employer Obligations," by Thomas P. Burke, Esq., and Daniel Weisberg, Esq. Reprinted with permission, Brobeck, Phlegler & Harrison.

PREVENTING VIOLENCE IN THE WORKPLACE

Charles E. Labig, Ph.D.

RHR International Co.

American Management Association

New York • Atlanta • Boston • Chicago • Kansas City • San Francisco • Washington, D.C.
Brussels • Mexico City • Tokyo • Toronto

This publication is designed to provide accurate and authoritative information in regard to the subject matter covered. It is sold with the understanding that the publisher is not engaged in rendering legal, accounting, or other professional service. If legal advice or other expert assistance is required, the services of a competent professional person should be sought.

Library of Congress Cataloging-in-Publication Data

Labig, Charles E.
        Preventing violence in the workplace / Charles E. Labig.
            p.   cm.
        Includes bibliographical references and index.
        ISBN 0-8144-0287-9
        1.   Violence in the workplace.   2.   Employee crimes--Prevention.
    3.   Violence--Forecasting.   I.   Title
    HF5549.5.E43L3   1995
    658.4'73--dc20   95-117
                                                                    CIP

Printing number

10   9   8   7   6   5   4   3   2

To
Andrew
Without whom this book would not have been written

Contents

9 Downsizing and Terminations   **153**

Effective Downsizing: Difficult but Possible •
Announcing the Bad News • Going On: Dealing
With the Survivors • A Company That Did It
Right: Best Practices

10 Conclusion   **181**

Appendix: Company Self-Assessment
Exercise   **185**

References   **191**

Index   **193**

PREVENTING VIOLENCE IN THE WORKPLACE

Chapter 1
Introduction

Violence in the workplace is the kind of subject we don't want to think about. We want to believe it happens only to other people. Most of the time we think that the victims of workplace violence are different from us, that their companies are on some different psychological or physical plane from ours. If we really begin to think about the possibility of serious violence where we work, we may become anxious and intensely uncomfortable. It is frightening to realize that we are so vulnerable to the whims and rages of others. These thoughts create the same reaction in us that we may have when we hear about carjackings. They happen only in places where we do not live, and to other people.

Yet hardly a week goes by without another newspaper headline or a television news report describing some crazed employee blowing away co-workers or supervisors. We hear of a "madman" entering a business with an automatic weapon and murdering whoever happens to have the misfortune of being there. The most recent twist on workplace violence focuses on an estranged spouse or ex-lover seeking reconciliation or revenge at the worksite.

In May 1993 a postal employee in Dearborn, Michigan, killed a co-worker and wounded his supervisor and the woman who got the job he wanted. The same day, another disgruntled worker, wearing a PSYCHO T-shirt, walked into a Dana Point, California, post office and killed a letter carrier and wounded a clerk. The two incidents occurred just hours apart. Two months later, nine people were shot dead at the high-rise offices of a prestigious law firm in San Francisco's financial district. In March 1994, three people at a Santa Fe Springs, California, were shot to death. In April 1994, a recently fired man walked into Sumitomo Electric Fiber Optics Corporation in Durham, North

Carolina, and killed two former bosses and wounded two others. These bloody episodes are prodding employers into action.

The Proliferation of Violence in the Workplace

The statistics on the frequency and seriousness of workplace violence are frightening. Workplace violence is the fastest growing type of murder in the United States, and it is increasing at an alarming rate. Four percent of all murders occur on the job. According to the National Institute for Occupational Safety and Health (NIOSH), homicide and other workplace violence has become the second leading cause of death in the workplace. The study reported that there were 1,063 work-related homicides in 1993—one third more than the annual rate during the 1980s and a 5.6 percent increase from 1992. Among those murdered, 177 were in managerial and professional occupations, 335 were in sales, 225 were in services, and 202 were drivers or factory workers. The annual rate at which bosses are being killed at work has doubled since 1985. Guns are the means in 75 percent of all deaths. And that is only the homicides. The Bureau of Labor Statistics has not kept track of violent assaults or threats in which no one dies. According to the president of Guardsmark, a national security company, on-the-job violence cost U.S. companies about $4.2 billion in 1992. What these data imply is that whatever your industry or level within a business, if you deal with the public or have employees, you cannot afford to avoid the issue of workplace violence.

The fact is that the workplace is becoming more dangerous. The number of workers killed annually on the job during all of the 1980s was 760. Of these, 12 percent were homicides, ranging from liquor store clerks murdered by an outside assailant to people killed by a fellow employee. The vast majority of victims, 80 percent, were male. Homicide was the leading cause of on-the-job fatalities for women. Forty-one percent of female deaths on the job are caused by homicide. Eighty-three percent of workplace victims are Caucasian, 10 percent African-American, 3 percent Latino, 3 percent Asian. Service and sales workers have the most work-related homicides, followed by executives, administrators, and managers. Thirty-six percent of victims are in retailing, 17 percent in service industries, and 11 percent in public administration, including law enforcement. According to NIOSH, the rate of occupational homicides per hundred thousand employees in the United States during the 1980–1988 period was 1.7 for retail trade and public administration; 1.5 for transport and communication, and public utilities; .69 for construction; .63 for services; .58 for agriculture, forestry, and fishing; .5 for mining; .39 for finance, insurance, and real estate; .27 for manufacturing; and .2 for wholesalers. While these rates are relatively low, they are growing at a rapid pace and, as the figures illustrate, cut across every type of business. In addition, for every homicide, there may be a dozen suicides, which have the same devastating effect as homicide on those who remain.

Even more shocking is the fact that homicide represents only the tip of the iceberg. The U.S. Department of Justice found that one of every six crimes occurs at work, with 1 million victims affected yearly. The Northwestern National Life Insurance Institute for Occupational Safety and Health released a study showing that one of four workers was harassed, threatened, or attacked on the job between July 1992 and July 1993. Nineteen percent of workers report being harassed on the job; 7 percent report threats of physical harm, and 3 percent report being physically attacked. The effect of this proliferation of violence on the job is taking its toll: 88 percent of workers say that they are psychologically affected, 62 percent say their work life is disrupted, 23 percent are physically injured or sick, and only 7 percent report no negative effect. Statistics can't begin to convey the level of human suffering and the damage inflicted by workplace violence on an affected company's workforce and on its public image.

For every workplace murder, there are scores of injuries, beatings, stabbings, suicides, shootings, rapes, psychological traumas, and mental health problems. In an American Management Association survey released in April 1994, more than half of 311 companies said that at least one of their workers had been attacked, threatened, or killed on the job in the past four years. Yet only one quarter of companies offered formal training to employees in coping with workplace violence, and only 11 percent offered training to all employees.

The Society for Human Resource Management has found that in addition to murder, other acts of violence have become more prevalent at work. More than one third of the 479 human resources professionals who responded to its survey said that people in their organizations have experienced violent acts. Thirty-two percent said that one or more violent acts have occurred since 1989, and more than 80 percent said that the acts took place since 1991. Among those reporting more than one altercation, 54 percent had between two and five violent workplace between 1989 and 1994. Although almost three quarters of the violent incidents were physical altercations, a frightening 17 percent were shootings, with one death reported. Eight percent were stabbings; 6 percent of these were sexual assaults. More than half (54 percent) of the violent incidents were committed by an employee against another employee; about 13 percent involved an employee against a supervisor; and 7 percent were committed by customers against employees.

What prompts violence at work? Although 36 percent of the respondents in the Society for Human Resource Management study could not pinpoint a specific reason, the remaining respondents cited a number of causes. The leading motives were personality conflicts (38 percent) and family and marital problems (15 percent). Other incidents were related to drug or alcohol abuse (10 percent), nonspecific stress (7.5 percent) and firings or layoffs (7 percent). Two percent of the violent acts were attributed to a violent criminal history.

In a more comprehensive study, the Northwestern National Life Insurance Institute for Occupational Safety and Health found various motives for workplace attacks: irrational behavior (26 percent); dissatisfaction with service (19 percent); interpersonal conflict (15 percent); upset at being disciplined (12 percent); criminal behavior (10 percent); personal problems (8 percent); firing or layoff (2 percent); and prejudice (1 percent). The cause of 7 percent of the attacks was unknown.

Growing Corporate Liability

If managers don't begin to address the problem of violence in the workplace, courts and regulatory systems will. Recently, a

Florida court of appeals ruled that Circle K Corporation was liable for failing to take action that might have prevented the murder of a twenty-seven-year-old clerk by a robber. Epidemiologists at the federal Center for Disease Control are exploring ways to expand government enforcement of corporate liability for violence. They believe that many workplace murders are preventable and therefore constitute a violation of the general duty clause of the Occupational Safety and Health Act (OSHA).

In January 1994, Assistant Secretary of Labor for Occupational Safety and Health Joseph Dear stated that it is now OSHA's policy to cite employers that fail to adequately protect their workers from acts of violence under Section 5(a) of the OSH Act, which requires employers to provide a place of employment free from recognized hazards likely to cause death or serious bodily harm. As of April 1994, there were at least five pending citations under the general duty clause for failure to protect workers from exposure to violence in the workplace.

Potential liability for violence in the workplace varies greatly, depending on the laws of the particular state in which the employer is located. Although an employer's liability has traditionally been limited by state workers' compensation laws, a number of courts have expanded an employer's duty to provide a safe workplace by permitting employees to bring suits under new common law tort theories, such as negligent hiring, negligent supervision, and negligent retention. Imagine losing a civil suit and hundreds of thousands or even millions of dollars because your company does not have the right supervision or training in place. Corporations without adequate preventive measures will find that they are particularly subject to lawsuits and huge settlements.

One victim's family sued the company after an employee had confided to his work supervisor that he was having difficulties at home and later killed several co-workers in the office. The case was settled for several hundred thousand dollars. Another employer was held liable for negligent hiring and supervision when its door attendant, who had been in previous fights, assaulted a patron. A church lost a case in which a ten-year-old parishioner was raped by an employee who had a recent conviction for child molestation because the court believed it was reasonably foreseeable that the employee's duties would bring him into contact with children. In another case, an employer of private guards was found liable for almost $1 million after one of the guards sexually assaulted a woman. The jury found that the employer failed to conduct a sufficiently detailed examination of job applicant's potential for violence in the hiring process. These cases illustrate the dramatic and consistent trend toward holding companies liable for the violent acts of their employees and the increased importance of assessment of violence potential by employers.

With the increase in frequency and severity of workplace violence, the number of lawsuits arising out of these incidents has increased at a roughly proportionate rate. While this area of the law is still evolving, judgments are consistently indicating that employers are going to be held accountable for failing to take actions to avoid being victimized by employee and customer violence. To avoid liability, employers will have to take measures to minimize the threat of violence to their employees and to respond appropriately and swiftly to any threats of violence as they become aware of them.

In almost all states, courts have ruled that employers have a duty of care toward their customers and employees to take reasonable steps to prevent violence on their premises and by their employees. Employers may be held liable for negligence in providing a reasonably safe workplace or for negligent hiring or supervision when a customer or an employee become violent. Companies that ignore the possibility of workplace violence clearly will do so at their own financial peril.

The Stereotype of the Mentally Ill Violent Person

Most of us know very little about the kind of person likely to be the perpetrator of such terror. The prevailing view is that they are a "certain kind of person," usually mentally ill and sometimes sociopathic. This perception is reinforced by the headlines that superficially describe these individual's paranoid thoughts and bizarre motivations. The fact of the matter is that there is not one type of person committing these violent acts. If we do not understand who the perpetrators really are, we can neither develop plans to prevent violence from occurring nor prepare to respond to crises as they arise.

Workplace violence is committed by many types of people, with differing sets of motives and in varying circumstances. I, too, once accepted the common stereotypes about the mentally ill and about normalcy. Almost twenty years ago, I was a young, idealistic student using doctoral study in psychology to figure out what really makes people behave the way they do and, in the process, trying to discover the key to happiness. Of course, the way psychology goes about teaching its disciples these lessons is to have them work with people who define themselves as unhappy or as mentally disturbed.

I will never forget my first visit to a state psychiatric hospital. I remember driving onto its grounds, its three-story, 1950-style rectangular brick buildings looming up in front of me. The first thing I noticed was how set off from the rest of the world it was, the iron gates at the front drive and its extending fences demarking a separate world. The second feature that jumped out at me was the bars on every window, the wire diamond-shaped kind. Once the car engine was shut off, muted cries and laughter could be heard from some of the windows. From others, there was only mysterious silence. Bodies shuffled along the walks, their legs and arms stiff from what I later learned were some of the serious side effects of antipsychotic medication. These were people who seemed fundamentally different, to be almost another species of being.

Over the next five years, I got to know many of these residents. I moved beyond my terror that their illnesses were somehow contagious—a deeply primitive but powerful fear that lurks just below consciousness in many people. I discovered that these patients were really much more like me than different. Eventually, I came to see that they are like all of us in most ways, except that they have serious malfunctioning in their brains. It is these biological misfirings and the medications used to treat them that create the strange thoughts and behaviors that arouse the primitive fears that intimidate us.

During this period I got to know some of the more famous residents of the institution. These were individuals with infamous pasts, mostly distinguished for murder or attempted murder. There was the man who had killed both of his parents and the man who used a machete to go after the drivers of other cars along a major highway. There was a woman who had strangled her lover while under the influence of drugs. A woman who had cut up another patient while she slept and then drank the blood described being abused as a child by a man from a cult who wore a black robe and hood and who kept appearing in her hospital room.

All of these people, and other patients with violent histories, had one thing in common: a set of perceptions, supported by their experiences, thoughts, and feelings, that they believed to be real and accurate. In the context of those perceptions, their violent acts made sense. Each perceived his course of action as the only logical option available, given his view of what the reality was. These were all people with genuine and severe mental illnesses. They had been psychotic, meaning that they had severely distorted the reality around them because of chemical malfunctions in their brains. They hallucinated; that is, they saw things that were not real presenting events but that were terrifying and dangerous. They heard voices that no one else heard and that threatened to injure or kill them. On the basis of their experience of reality, they struck out in order to protect themselves and to calm their overwhelming feelings of terror.

People like the patients I just described, who suffer from severe mental illness, are similar to one kind of person who commits workplace violence, except that these patients are at later stages of their illnesses. Typically, it is in the earliest or acute stages of their illnesses that these individuals present risk in the workplace. As far as we know at this point in the evolution of our knowledge of mental illness, events in their lives that are sufficiently stressful set off psychotic processes, such as hallucinations (hearing voices or seeing things that are not real) and delusions (beliefs without a foundation in reality). This can happen because these people have physiological weaknesses or predispositions, probably in the chemical processors in the nerve endings of their brains. Once these patients' distorted experiences and perceptions are understood, it becomes clear that their behavior is consistent with how most of us act.

Most of the general public believe that it is those who are the mentally ill who cause most of the violence that occurs in the workplace. In fact, it is unlikely that this group of people represents even the majority of those who commit workplace violence.

At the next step in my career, I developed a crisis intervention and evaluation unit for an outpatient community mental health center, which was designed to serve "normal" people. I found myself confronted with another group of persons with histories of violence. Most of these individuals did not have a diagnosable mental illness. What they did have was a view of reality that was pessimistic. They carried a personal collection of stories of hurt, rejection, and powerlessness. Sometimes, they were burdened by large chips on their shoulders. Some were quietly depressed. Others had an air of desperation; many felt as if they were about to explode. What they shared in common was a shortage of internal or external resources, which left them feeling unable to cope with the abundance of stressful demands in their lives.

A hundred years ago, one of the founders of modern psychological thinking, Sigmund Freud, wrote that there are two important aspects to life: loving and working. Many of my outpatient clients suffered significantly in both arenas. There were schoolchildren unable to concentrate because of emotional distress, such as loneliness or parental rejection, whose truancy and aggression were cries for help. There were men who had never experienced sufficient affirmation from others to feel confident about themselves. Because of this, they were afraid to risk trying to develop the skills that are necessary to be successful in life. Instead, they resorted to continually bullying and intimidating others to prove that they were "real men." We also saw the women who were their wives or girlfriends, often after a beating or a threat that had brought the police. These women felt powerless and desperate. There were also the women who were so needy that they resorted to threatening to harm themselves and sometimes even cut themselves to get the attention they so desperately sought.

There was one group of individuals who were particularly frightening. They were mostly court-connected, either on probation or with restraining orders issued against them. Some had committed antisocial acts, like fighting or stealing. Some had assaulted their wives or girlfriends. What was common to the group was that they had little remorse for what they had done and blamed others for all of their problems. They often seemed at war with the rest of humanity but without a clear objective for victory. What was so frightening was that most lacked anything resembling a conscience. They were prepared to do literally anything to justify their impulsive behavior. The worst example was a man who had been convicted of raping a woman as she lay dying after he had slit her throat. He was living in a prison halfway house and was seeking outpatient psychotherapy as part of a strategy to be placed on parole. He blamed the woman for what he had done to her. It was all her fault. There was nothing he wanted to change about himself. Some of these people came as close as anyone I ever saw to being a "violent-type personality." They didn't care about anyone but themselves. They were fairly impulsive and eager to settle conflicts at the most basic physical level of battle. What keeps me from stereotyping them as violent, however, is that many of them held regular jobs for many years without any incidences of disturbance at the worksite.

When I returned to the state hospital system, I supervised sixteen psychologists who evaluated hospitalized persons for the courts to determine if the patients were competent to stand trial or able to be held criminally responsible for the criminal behavior with which they were charged or convicted. These evaluations could fill a textbook with all their descriptions of people who had lost control and acted in violent ways. Charges ranged from assault to arson to murder. Many people we saw had lived apparently normal lives until something had shifted. There had been a sudden change or provocation that led to their striking out. Like those who commit workplace violence, these individuals were motivated by a desire for revenge or a need to seek relief from unbearable pressures. They always felt trapped in bad circumstances and could find no way out. Their thinking always was that violence represented their only viable alternative.

Later in my career, but before the downsizings of the 1980s,

I explored another part of humanity through an employee assistance program (EAP) that I developed and ran for a number of different companies. An EAP is an in-house or contracted counseling program. Many companies have resorted to these as they've realized the significant price they are paying in lower productivity and quality for their workers' personal and work problems. Through this work, I again discovered that people are more alike than different. The people with whom I worked were not marginal or just barely getting by. They were mostly successful businesspeople, stuck in their careers, entwined in serious problems with a boss, struggling with personal relationships, or trying to figure out what was missing in their lives that was leaving them feeling unhappy. Most were doing their best to contribute and succeed at work. Some harbored serious resentments toward their companies, feeling that their hard work and loyalty were not being rewarded. They thought that their bosses were, at worst, biased against them or, at best, having trouble "connecting." On the basis of these experiences, I do not have to be convinced of the central importance of work in most people's lives or of the severe distress that work problems can create. I saw executives at the highest levels of major corporations who were internally and secretly out of control. They had learned to cope with the pressures of work by drinking excessively or by making decisions that would later blow up in their faces. Some had sacrificed their personal lives so totally for work that they were left in a shambles.

What do all of these individuals and groups have in common? Given the right set of circumstances and events, they match the people who have become violent in the workplace.

Is there a way to know which of these people will be tomorrow's newspaper headline? I believe that there is, but it is not as simple as many people say. In fact, I believe that most of the people I have just described could have become violent, given the right stresses and responses by those around them.

The Prevailing Myth of a Violent Personality Type

A second prevailing myth suggests the existence of a specific type of person out there, waiting to explode into violence at the worksite. If this were true, all we would have to do to prevent violence is define these individual's characteristics and see that we either do not hire or do not retain them at our company.

Some writers and lecturers present composite pictures of the person who will become violent at work—a white male, about forty years of age, with a history of violence. He owns several guns or has a preoccupation with them. He is angry but lacks an available or acceptable target for expressing his anger. He has a history of interpersonal conflict, including family or marital problems. He is an introvert and is socially withdrawn. He may have had some serious emotional difficulties in the past that led him to receive some kind of professional help. He has a pattern of becoming withdrawn and sometimes of complaining excessively to management. Others often describe him as paranoid and self-destructive.

There are two major problems with this kind of typecasting. Because it is terribly simplistic, it may lead businesspeople to overlook or underestimate the potential for violence in other kinds of individuals who, in reality, are just as likely to explode. Companies cannot afford to create a false sense of security for themselves. The second problem with typecasting is that violence is not the result of a trait that an individual has. It is not because you are a certain kind of person that you are likely to become violent at work. Workplace violence is situational. It always occurs as part of a sequence of events and circumstances, only part of which is determined by the personality of the individual perpetrator.

Workplace violence is the result of many factors all converging at the wrong time and at the wrong place. Violence results from the anger of disgruntled employees, from the accessibility of a business to the public (e.g., hospital emergency rooms and retail stores), and from the rage of relatives or friends such as jilted lovers or estranged spouses. It appears to be caused by many things. Not the least of these may be the loss of society's support structures, often the result of decreased participation in church or temple, disruption of family and marriage through divorce or geographic relocation, and reductions in social support programs for those in need. All of these losses make people more vulnerable to viewing work as the key avenue to feeling valued and important, to belonging, and to finding meaning in their lives. What makes this situation so dangerous is that while the importance of work is growing for many people, the pressure to perform well there in order to retain their jobs has increased greatly. Meanwhile, people feel left with fewer resources to fall back on.

Is workplace violence an inevitable result of the epidemic of violence in our society, or are there actions that can actually prevent or lower the probability of its occurrence? Regardless of how we view the causes of increased violence in the workplace, such violence is increasing rapidly and must be addressed. Only with increased understanding of how and with whom it occurs can we develop preventive measures to protect companies and their employees.

The fact is that there are no simple answers to questions about about who commits workplace violence. Some perpetrators are mentally ill, but many are not. The perpetrators of violence tend to fall into groups that have some characteristics in common, but they also have significant individual differences. Many of the people who become violent, who create the headlines that leave you and me shaking our heads in disbelief and fear, are generally more like us than they are different. In spite of our limited ability to predict who will ultimately act in a violent manner, we know quite a lot about the spiraling process that leads up to violence in the workplace, the circumstances and environment that make it more likely, and the methods that can keep the process from beginning or de-escalate it when it does occur.

This book is an effort to educate the business community about the all-too-mysterious topic of workplace violence and about all of the different types of situations, motives, and people who bring it about. The book is designed not to make you a psychologist but to help you become well enough informed to develop the policies and to deal with the professionals you need in order to protect yourself, your company, and its employees from the growing epidemic of workplace violence.

Chapter 2 presents our most advanced psychological understanding of how violence is produced. It discusses the best way to predict violence or to assess its risk in a particular situation.

This state-of-the-art model, while detailed, is the basis for under-standing what will be effective or will fail in every aspect of violence prevention and control. Chapter 3 describes the various sources or circumstances around which workplace violence oc-curs, because each carries its own set of motives, needs, and solutions. Chapter 4 discusses hiring and selection issues, since most companies seek a way to avoid hiring high-risk individuals. Chapter 5 is contributed by one of the leading legal experts in employment law in the nation. Garry Mathiason writes about the most common legal mistakes companies make in handling issues with potential for violence. Chapter 6 describes the poli-cies and procedures your company needs in order to reduce its risk for workplace violence. Chapter 7 explains how to develop a violence response team. Should a threat of violence occur, having such a team will prepare your company to deal with it quickly and effectively in a way that de-escalates the situation before it can become violent. Chapter 8 describes the many changes occurring in the workplace that make violence more likely to occur. It discusses the organizational dynamics that corporate leaders can develop to mitigate the risk of violence and at the same time improve morale, productivity, and service. Chapter 9 deals specifically with how to handle downsizing and termina-tions. These are two of the circumstances most readily identified as likely to provoke violence. Chapter 10 summarizes some of the key issues in the book. It points out some considerations by which to evaluate how your company is dealing with the threat of workplace violence. Chapter 11 presents an assessment instru-ment you can take yourself or give to your staff to measure your company's current readiness to prevent violence and to identify important areas for improvement and taking preventive action.

The Problem of Denial

In order to be able to use this book productively, you must face one major challenge—dealing with your own emotions. Work-place violence is an emotional topic. Most of us have strong emotional reactions to the subjects of violence and work, and dealing with these reactions is an essential element in prevention.

As I travel across the United States discussing violence in the workplace, I hear two kinds of reactions from businesspeople. Many managers ask about how to get their companies' chief executive officers to take the issue of workplace violence seriously. They say that when they have attempted to bring up the subject, they find their bosses closed to any discussion of the topic. Sometimes this avoidance is coupled with statements like: "There aren't any of that kind of employee at our company." I personally received a similar response at a presentation I made to a senior group of human resources managers from some of the nation's largest companies. Many of the participants appeared to have a difficult time taking the subject seriously. Their response seemed to reflect both the pressures they faced from their presidents and CEOs in other areas and their own discomfort with the topic.

The second common reaction is what may be characterized best as near-panic. This seems to be more prevalent at middle and lower layers of organizations and in people who are experiencing firsthand the threats and dangers of potential violence. Many seminar attendees describe situations in which their employees have overreacted to individual side comments or rumors by attributing too much importance to them. This has resulted in the employees' jumping to take action too quickly without getting sufficient facts first, thereby making some serious mistakes.

Be they factory workers, salespeople, or executives, most people do not understand the causes of workplace violence or what leads up to it occurring. When they hear about it, they either oversimplify it, avoid the topic by not taking it seriously, or conclude that violence is random and therefore not preventable. Like the violence on the street that appears to be so senseless and inexplicable, this ambiguity leaves them feeling very vulnerable and fearful.

The natural human response to a phenomenon that seems beyond one's ability to understand or control is to use the psychological defense of denial—to pretend that "it can't happen here." This has been the most typical response of corporate senior executives. Only when something happens across the street do they realize their vulnerability. Denial can be very dangerous because it decreases the likelihood that measures to prevent violence and to prepare to respond quickly and effectively to high-risk situations will be put into place. Such denial is genuine folly in the context of statistics showing a rapid increase in the frequency of serious violence in the workplace. In the United States, two dozen employees kill their superiors each year, compared to about twelve a year in the 1970s. There are now more than 2 million assaults annually in the workplace. Six million American workers are threatened and 16 million harassed each year.

One owner of a manufacturing company said: "You're vulnerable. You never know as an executive whether an employee will snap and take a shot at you. That's the scary part of being a boss." As violence in the workplace becomes a terrifying possibility, businesses have begun taking a more proactive approach in preventing it. Klaussner Furniture Industries in Asheboro, North Carolina, is an example of a company that has taken a proactive stance to avoid violence through an improved complaint procedure, an in-house employee assistance program, and a quick response to any behavior (e.g., hitting, slapping, or harassing) that could escalate into more serious violence. The problem is immediately resolved through a process of separation, communication, and, if needed, suspension.

Violence does not occur in a vacuum. It is the result of an escalating process, rather than of one sudden event. Facing the issue of possible workplace violence by anticipating and preparing for it can make it much less likely to occur. The cost of denying the possibility of violence within a company grows daily as corporations continue to lose civil lawsuits that expand the range and limits of their liability and as juries hold companies and their executives liable for larger and larger financial settlements. In addition, there are terrible effects from workplace violence; it both disrupts operations and has a negative effect on public relations.

The purpose of this book is to get beyond denial. There are many things that can be done to lower the probability of violence within a company. If people can understand who commits violence, the circumstances that lead them to it, and the preventive measures that can be taken, the growing epidemic of workplace violence can be controlled. With all of the other assaults on U.S. industry and its workforce from intensifying global competition, here is one arena where a company can create real competitive advantage for itself and its employees.

Chapter 2

The Spiral That Leads to Workplace Violence

Workplace violence is not well understood or researched for two reasons. First, it is a fairly recent phenomenon and has occurred in relatively low numbers overall, so sufficient statistical information is not available to permit definitive conclusions about causes, predictions, or solutions. Second, many companies that have experienced workplace violence are involved in related litigation for up to a decade after the event. This situation makes them unwilling to share much information about what happened and thus limits how much companies can learn from one another.

Given these limitations, this chapter discusses our most advanced knowledge of the psychology of the individuals who commit workplace violence. The model presented here represents the current state of our ability to predict who will act violently and provides the basis for assessing the risk for violence of a particular individual. It describes our level of understanding about the process that leads to workplace violence through an escalating spiral of events and reactions by an individual within his or her environment. By understanding these basic processes, you will be able to plan and evaluate the most appropriate preventive measures for your company. You may also increase your knowledge about how to motivate, manage, and lead people in the corporate environment.

Most people believe that there are violent individuals in the world and that if we could just identify who they are, we could protect ourselves from them by not hiring them. Nothing in the behavioral or social sciences supports this belief. The model of prediction described here is a situational one, not one based on traits or personality alone. It has been developed through research and clinical use over fifteen years by John Monahan, a psychologist at the University of Virginia Law School. It is the best generic model available to describe the mental and behavioral cycle and the particular set of circumstances that escalate over time into violence.

This cycle or spiral has four parts:

1. It begins when an individual encounters an event that he experiences as stressful.
2. The person reacts to this event with certain kinds of thoughts to which he is predisposed by his personality.
3. These thoughts lead to emotional responses.
4. These responses in turn determine the behavior that the individual will use to respond to the situation.

This cycle continues as other people in the individual's environment respond to the individual's behavior in a way that increases or decreases the person's experience of stress, and the cycle repeats itself. If the environment increases the person's stress, reactive thoughts and emotions are likely to be intensified and to lead to escalating behaviors. It can reach a point where the person comes to believe that violence is the only viable, if desperate, way to cope with the situation or to relieve unbearable distress and that he must therefore respond with violence. The responses of those around the person, including family members, co-workers, and supervisors, can either de-escalate the likelihood of violence or push the person over the edge.

This model fits the available data about persons who have committed workplace violence. Workplace violence is never a sudden event. Typically, the person has given frequent and repeated warnings that he was going to be violent. People in the individual's world have responded or failed to respond in ways that contributed to the outcome. Violence in the workplace starts with an individual's experiencing events as stressful. A series of internal and external events then escalates into headlines.

If you comprehend the nature of the cycle that spirals into violence, you will be far ahead in understanding how your company can effectively prevent workplace violence. In addition, it will help you make sense and manage the myriad providers and vendors who are trying to sell you programs or services to deal with potential violence in your company.

A Model of How Violence Occurs and How to Predict It

Workplace violence, as I have said, grows out of a cycle of events and responses. Recognizing and understanding this cycle is essential to preventing such violence as an outcome.

Stress: The Precipitating Event

Step 1 in the cycle that leads to violence is the occurrence of a stressful event in a person's life. The concept of stress is central to understanding violence; it is one of the organizing issues in violence prediction. Stress is defined as a state of imbalance between the demands of a person's social and physical environment and that person's ability to cope with those demands. The higher the ratio of demands to resources, the greater the stress. Stress is not an objective event; that is, you cannot measure it by knowing the facts about a person's situation. Rather, stress is an internal condition dependent on the individual's subjective experience of her situation. What one person perceives as stressful may be taken by another person as challenging and stimulating. The difference between the two reactions lies in the individual's perceptions, beliefs, and emotions about the situation.

Stressful events can include frustrations, annoyances, power struggles, insults, threats, assaults by others, or job changes, including disciplinary actions and termination. They are anything that the individual sees as a demand or as threatening in any way to her well-being. A challenging event becomes stressful when a person is not sure she has the resources to respond successfully to the demand. The event is then taken as a threat rather than as an opportunity.

How much an event triggers a response of feeling stressed

or threatened in a person is determined by how she thinks and feels about the event. These thoughts and feelings, in turn, direct her to react to these events with particular responses.

Thoughts: The First Response

Step 2 in the violence cycle comes as the person reacts to the stressful event with certain kinds of thoughts to which he is predisposed by his personality. These thoughts are filtered through certain cognitive or thought processes and are of two types: appraisals and expectations.

An *appraisal* is the way a person interprets an event or gives meaning to it. One type of appraisal has to do with deciding whether the event is of any importance. Whether an individual perceives an event as having no consequence or as being very important and even critical to his basic well-being makes a tremendous difference in how stressful it is and in how the person responds to it. Another type of appraisal has to do with what intentionality, if any, is attributed to an event. If it is believed that other people involved in creating an event have a particular set of motives and thus are acting in a deliberate fashion, the reasons behind the event are going to determine the person's response more than the event itself. Individuals can have many different ways of appraising the same event, and these different interpretations lead them to react with entirely different emotions and levels of intensity. How a person thinks about an event is determined by many things. In part, it is framed by the facts of the event, its circumstances, how people act (the tone of their voice and body language as well as what they say), the nature of the individuals involved, and the person's past experiences with those people. To a great degree, however, a person's thoughts about or appraisals of an event are a reflection of his own mental processes, which are determined by his temperament and by the central life experiences that have shaped his personality and influenced him to think, feel, and act as he does.

Expectations, the second type of response, are the thoughts a person has about what will happen because of a particular event and what effect his actions can have on that outcome. Here is an example of how expectations work: I believe that my supervisor has just spoken with me about my lack of cooperation with my work group because he is building a case for firing me because he's never liked me (my appraisal of his intentions). I believe that the only way I can foil his plan and protect myself from being terminated is to threaten him with bodily harm (my judgment about what I expect will happen and what I have to do to get the outcome I desire). Therefore, it becomes likely that I will threaten my supervisor. In contrast, if I expect that by becoming more cooperative and acting in a somewhat acquiescent manner I can bring my supervisor around so that he will not fire me, then I will probably respond in an entirely different way. I might behave in a more friendly and responsive manner, which will certainly be free of any kind of threats. One set of appraisals and expectations sets the stage for confrontation, escalation, and possible violence. The other way of thinking makes violence unlikely.

Expectations and appraisals form the thought processes that a person uses to interpret and react to events around him. While they may be altered to some degree by events, people's expectations and appraisals tend to be fairly consistent over time and are a reflection of their beliefs, of how they have come to see the world. These cognitive factors predispose people toward or inhibit violent behavior.

The tendency to blame other people for things that go wrong and always to hold oneself completely blameless for problems is one of the strongest cognitive predisposers towards violence. If I think that most people are out to harm me or that the best way to get what I want is to bully and intimidate, then I am more likely to interpret the behavior of other people as threatening and to act in such a way as to escalate situations than is someone who is more comfortable with other people's motives. Violent delusions and fantasies are extreme forms of this way of thinking. For example, if I have a delusion that you are deliberately trying to make me lose my job as part of a conspiracy to destroy me and conclude that the only way I can protect myself is to eliminate you, then that is what I will try to do.

On the other hand, if I have a different set of beliefs about people and about how to get the results I want, I may be predisposed away from thinking, feeling, or acting in ways that could lead to violence. Examples of these kind of violence-inhibiting thought processes are thinking of myself as a peace-loving, reasonable, and kind person who always gives others the benefit of the doubt and thinking that others do the best they can and have good intentions and honest motives. Inhibiting expectations connect escalation and violence with undesirable outcomes. Two examples of inhibiting thinking are believing that I will always get caught and punished when I do something wrong or break the rules and believing that if I stand up to other people in a demanding way, they will not like me and I will get hurt or at least not get my way.

Sometimes, although an employee may be expressing threatening or violent thoughts, employers make the mistake of judging that a person is not dangerous because she is not acting in a highly emotional way. A person does not have to become emotionally aroused to become violent. In other words, you cannot depend on a person's expressing volatile emotions to make you aware that a violent incident may occur. While it is more common for thoughts to lead to certain emotional reactions before an individual erupts into action, this is not always the case. Just thinking about a stressful event in a way that defines it as intensely, immediately, and sufficiently threatening can cause some people to move directly to taking desperate measures.

The Emotional Reaction

Step 3 in the cycle has to do with emotions. An individual's emotional reactions come from two sources. One is the way the person has thought about the stressful event. The second is the person's temperament or disposition. People tend to have typical or habitual ways of responding emotionally to different situations.

As with appraisals and expectations in thinking, emotions come in two different types as they relate to violence. Emotions either help predispose a person toward becoming violent or help inhibit a person from becoming violent. Emotional reactions that make it more likely that a person will become violent in reaction to a stressful situation are anger, hatred, blame, and terror. People who typically react emotionally in these ways are at higher risk of escalating into violence. Emotional reactions can also intervene to inhibit an individual's behavior. Empathy and guilt make it less likely that a person will strike out. When a person is aware of the impact her actions would have on another person, and when she has a sense of the hurt those actions could create, her emotions can do one of two things. They can stop her from acting in such a hurtful way, or they can require that the thoughts and emotions pushing toward being violent become more intense before action is taken.

Sometimes emotional reactions can be stimulated simply by the emotional tone with which a person is addressed. A loud, intense, and menacing voice can create an instantaneous emotional response in certain people. This is all it takes to push some people into retaliatory action. Intense or intimidating body language can have the same impact. Generally, the more emotionally calm and safe an individual feels, the less likely he is to become violent. The more frightening and threatening he finds his environment, the more likely he is to respond with violence.

Taking Action: Violence or Avoidance

A person's thinking and emotional reactions lead to step 4 in the cycle toward violence: action. Think of this as the person's attempt to cope with the stressful event as it was experienced, interpreted, and reacted to within that individual. He then takes whatever actions make sense, based on his appraisals, expectations, and emotional reactions. The action responses will be attempts to regain control or to master the demands that the individual is experiencing as the source of his stress. If I am feeling at risk of losing my job, my behavior will be an attempt to reassure myself that that won't happen and to do whatever it takes to convince those who have control over my job of it as well.

People tend to respond at stage 4 in one of two ways: They fight or they withdraw and avoid. The type of response I choose will likely influence whether the original event is resolved or creates additional or new stress. If I believe that the only way to deal with the challenge I am experiencing is to assert my control or power by threatening to striking out physically, I will do so. If the boss with whom I am dealing responds in kind, it is likely that the situation will escalate. I will go through the cycle of thought processes, emotional reactions, and coping behaviors all over again. Each time I go through the cycle, I and those around me will have the opportunity to de-escalate or intensify the stress I experience. Whether a response attenuates or exacerbates the stress I experience decreases or increases my potential for violence. Sometimes, a lack of response can be as stress-inducing as a loud and threatening one. A large brokerage firm once decided to terminate the employment of one of its brokers. He was summarily called into his boss's office and fired. The company was unaware that this well-educated, always steady and calm man had wrapped up his entire life in his work. Losing his job was the most severe blow he could have suffered. According to news reports, he received no clear explanation of why he was being terminated; nor did he argue with his boss. The next day he got a gun and shot his boss dead. Sometimes what is *not* said creates the most stress.

It is sometimes difficult to discern what actions can be taken to reduce an employee's stress. For instance, when someone is experiencing a lot of distress on the job, you might think that transferring her to another worksite would provide a solution. The possibility that she might interpret the change as a victory for someone else at her expense may not be obvious. The result, however, may be more distressing than continuing the employee at the same worksite. Quitting a job may decrease or increase the stress a person is feeling. You cannot know which solution is right, which will increase or decrease an employee's stress level, without understanding his thinking and emotional processes.

Assessing the Risk for Violence

The assessment of an individual for risk of violence is a complicated process. To further illustrate Dr. Monahan's research about how violence occurs, here are the ten questions that he recommends you or your experts ask about every potentially violent situation you encounter as part of determining if there is a risk of violence:

1. What events precipitated the question of the person's potential for violence, and in what context did these events take place? From the very beginning, it is important to be clear about precisely what the person did or is alleged to have done that raised someone's concern about violence and its social context. Knowing exactly who said or did what provides clues to the situational context in which the person might react violently. The description of the aggressor in action is often the most valuable single source of information.

2. What are the person's relevant demographic characteristics? Certain individual characteristics are associated in a negative or positive way with violent behavior.

3. What is the person's history of violent behavior? Past episodes of violence tend to be one of the best predictors of future violence. This information can be elicited by asking such questions as "What is the most violent thing you have ever done?" or "What is the closest you have ever come to being violent?" Once a person has acted in a certain way, he is less inhibited about repeating it.

4. How similar are the past contexts in which the person has used violent coping mechanisms to the contexts in which the person likely will function in the future?

5. What is the base rate of violent behavior among individuals of this person's background? "Base rate" is a statistical term that refers to the frequency of violence within certain identifiable categories. It is the most significant single piece of statistical information used in making a prediction. At present these statistics are not readily available, making this question difficult to answer. As workplace violence continues to increase, base rates of violence at work can be established from company incident reports and from shared industry data.

6. What are the sources of stress in the person's current environment?

7. What cognitive (thought) and emotional factors indicate that the person may be predisposed to cope with stress in a violent manner?

8. What cognitive and affective factors indicate that the per-

son may be predisposed to cope with stress in a nonviolent manner?

9. In particular, who are the likely victims of the person's violence, and how accessible are they?

10. What means does the person possess to commit violence? If a gun or other lethal weapon is readily available and the person knows how to use it, she is obviously more at risk than someone without such access.

One other major factor must be taken into account in looking at the spiral that results in violence: substance abuse. An individual who is intoxicated or high on drugs is less inhibited and therefore more likely to act on the basis of initial thoughts or emotional reactions. In addition, substance abuse can impair a person's judgment, making it more difficult for him to think out alternative solutions or consider realistically what the consequences of his actions might be. Substance abuse can also interfere with emotions, reshaping a person's feelings about a stressful situation and making him more angry, anxious, or depressed and hopeless.

Substance abuse can play a major role in disinhibiting people's behavior. Many illegal drugs and inappropriate use of alcohol simply make an individual more likely to act impulsively. This disinhibition can contribute significantly to the escalation process and can be a key indicator that danger is ahead. Substance abuse is present in many situations involving workplace violence. Sometimes the employee is using the substance as a sedative or as an escape. In either case, it can simply be an attempt to deal with overwhelming stress.

Mental Illness and Violent Behavior

Because many people associate the warning signs and symptoms of people who become violent on the job with mental illness, they often ask whether they can decrease the incidence of violence in their company by not hiring or retaining persons who are mentally ill.

According to Dr. Monahan, there is a common perception that mental illness is connected to violence. He points to the fact that when 17 percent of prime time television programs depicted a mentally ill person, the persons were portrayed as violent 73 percent of the time, whereas "normal" characters were violent 4 percent of the time. Twenty-three percent of mentally ill characters were portrayed as homicidal, compared to 10 percent of "normal" characters. Clearly, the common stereotype is that the mentally ill are more violent. Here are the facts:

The latest studies show that 10 to 40 percent of mentally ill patients commit physical assault shortly before hospitalization, and 27 percent of released patients report at least one violent act within four months after discharge. But this may be a function of the type of patients selected for hospitalization, the nature and duration of treatment during hospitalization, and the risk assessment cutoff for discharge of patients from hospitals.

The rate of mental illness among prison inmates is high. One study shows that the rate of schizophrenia is three times higher among those in prison than among the population at large, that the rate of bipolar disorder (also known as manic-depressive illness) is seven to fourteen times higher, and that the prevalence of severe disorders is three to four times higher than on the outside.

Data suggest that, whether the measure is the prevalence of violence among the disordered or the prevalence of disorder among the violent, whether the sample is people who are selected for treatment as inmates, patients in institutions, or people randomly chosen from the open community, and no matter how many social and demographic factors are taken into account statistically, there appears to be a relationship between mental disorder and violent behavior. Mental disorder may be a significant risk factor for the occurrence of violence.

Monahan concludes, however, that it is only people currently experiencing psychotic symptoms who may be at increased risk for violence. Ninety percent of the mentally disordered are not violent. In addition, it may be that the victim's manner of reacting or overreacting to the "fear-inducing" aspects of the behavior of the person who is mentally ill that is the determining factor in the person's becoming violent. The data underscore the need for readily available mental health resources for those with psychotic symptoms.

How Good Are We at Predicting Violence?

How good is anyone at predicting violent behavior in others? The answer to this question has important implications for setting up a company violence prevention program. While the model you have just been introduced to is the best one available and points to the questions that need to asked, we need to consider how well any of the current models can predict violent behavior. Because it is a relatively new phenomenon, research on predicting workplace violence is based on the study of risk assessment in other contexts where prediction has been an issue for many decades, such as making civil commitments to mental hospitals, determining prison sentences, and granting parole.

Studies on risk prediction have isolated five facts about the accuracy of predicting violence:

1. Predictions based on direct clinical judgments of potential violence, self-reports, and collateral reports of community violence, are more accurate than those based on any one source of information.
2. Clinical judgment of risk for violence has been undervalued in previous research, meaning that clinical judgment is of some value.
3. Nonetheless, clinicians remain relatively inaccurate predictors of violence.
4. Clinical predictions of violence can be improved upon.
5. The prevalence of violence among women patients is underestimated. The cues that distinguish which women will become violent often go unnoticed, which elevates the risk of violence.

Overall, it is difficult to predict violence. With a labor force of 125 million and an annual rate of fewer than fifty employee-caused homicides, the annual base rate of employee homicide is one in 7 million. While accurate prediction of an event with such a low base rate is impossible, employers neither should or legally will be allowed to ignore workplace violence. In fact, this statistic points to the need for companies to be overly cautious in their risk assessments. It means that they must not rely too quickly on one clinician's judgment or take any warnings or particular groups for granted. When confronted with a risk situation, companies must gather as much data from as many different sources as possible as part of their risk assessment procedures. Finally, because it is so difficult to predict who will actually become violent in the workplace, companies must make every economically feasible effort to prevent violence from developing.

Chapter 3

Sources of Workplace Violence

There are six common sources of violence on the job:

1. Strangers, who typically are involved in the commission of a crime, such as robbery, or who have a grudge against the business
2. Current or past customers
3. Current and former co-workers who commit murders
4. Current and former co-workers who threaten and assault
5. Spouses or lovers involved in domestic disputes
6. Those infatuated with or who stalk employees

The best method of preventing violence varies depending on which of these contexts is involved. In this chapter we consider each context, using some real individuals to illustrate what we know about the situations that most commonly lead to violence on the job.

Strangers: Robbers and Grudge Holders

By far the vast majority of murders on the job are committed by strangers. Of the 1,063 homicides on the job in 1993, most were committed by strangers. Only forty-eight people were killed by co-workers and twenty by spouses. The actual number of stranger homicides may be higher, because the numbers I have just given include only immediate deaths, not trauma leading to death later on.

Factors that increase risk of a person's being killed in the workplace by a stranger are:

- Exchanging money with the public
- Working alone or with only a few others
- Working late-night or early-morning hours
- Working in high-crime areas
- Guarding valuable property or possessions
- Working in community settings

Anyone who handles cash and works alone becomes a target.

The immediate measures an employer can take to reduce the risk of violence for its employees in this situation primarily involve improving environmental surroundings and physical security. Companies can make high-risk areas visible to more people, install good external lighting, use drop safes to minimize cash on hand, and post signs stating that limited cash is on hand. OSHA recommends installing client alarms and surveillance cameras, increasing the number of staff on duty, providing training in conflict resolution and nonviolent response, and having police routinely patrol the worksite area.

Whether you own a small retail shop or work in a large corporation, physical facilities and environmental design need to be secure. Begin with assessing your security systems. Do you have a way to communicate quickly with your employees or the police if you need help? Do you have a backup communication system if your phones are damaged? You need to have a system that controls former employees' access to the worksite. Have you taken steps to control access of the public to work areas? Often, something simple and inexpensive can help. Changing the position of a cash register behind a counter relative to the doors—to make it look less accessible or vulnerable—or putting up a sign indicating that only a small amount of cash is kept on hand late at night can make a difference in the psychological perceptions of a potential robber, making him hesitate and even go elsewhere. Banks are no longer the only companies that have panic buttons on the desks or counters of particularly vulnerable staff. Every way that you limit the exposure of your employees physically makes you less liable and better protected.

If you use an external security firm, be sure to pick one that trains its employees well. The security industry is known for its high employee turnover rate. You want a company that has guards who are properly prepared and who have the right attitudes. They need to take the approach that the best security doesn't wait to react to a crisis. They get out and meet employees, find out what is happening, and are visible and approachable. They may also be a useful resource for training you and your employees about how to respond during a robbery or other crisis. Train employees to recognize and deal with strangers who gain access to the building during business hours; knowing how to do this could save your life or those of your employees.

Have you considered whether your products or services antagonize any particular groups or individuals? Are you receiving mail or phone calls complaining about your business? If so, you may want to protect yourself proactively by trying to reshape the public's feelings about you or at least to alter any false perceptions they may have about what you do.

Current and Past Customers

Working with the public has become increasingly dangerous. Hospital emergency rooms have become so violent that California has mandated training in violence prevention beginning in 1995. The situation is so bad that some hospital doctors and nurses have resorted to turning their name tags upside down to avoid being identified by potentially dangerous patients. A 1991 study by Pennsylvania State University of 1,209 emergency room nurses found nearly one in four had been confronted by people with weapons. Two thirds of those surveyed said they had been physically assaulted at least once, more than one third in the past year alone.

I was on a CNN television program with one of three doctors who had been shot in February 1993 at the Los Angeles County USC Medical Center. The man convicted of wounding the doctors in the rampage was a forty-one-year-old, skid-row loner named Ybarra Torres. He admitted attacking the physicians because he believed they had injected him with the virus that causes AIDS and then repeatedly referred him to a mental health unit when he returned seeking treatment for the resulting physical illnesses. He was sentenced to three life sentences for attempted murder, even though the jury agreed that he suffered from persecutory delusions. They concluded that he was rational enough to methodically plan and execute his crime. He had a thirty-four point plan for how he would carry out his attack. This shooting raised concerns over security in busy medical facilities.

Whether it is a hospital, a law firm, a brokerage house, or a McDonald's, it is clearly no longer sufficient to simply provide services to your customers. If you are in the retail or service industry, you must pay attention to the warning signs of potential violence in your customers. To accomplish this, you will have to spend enough time with them to understand how they experience the interaction they are having with you. In a 7-Eleven store, this may consist of simply monitoring customer behavior by paying attention to anything out of the ordinary, like someone hanging around a lot. It may require looking customers in the face while you give them change to assess their stability.

Dealing with potentially dangerous customers typically offers a higher level of control and preventive capability than dealing with strangers. You may still use all of the physical security tactics involved in preventing violence from strangers, but you have one additional resource at hand. If you take the time to get to know your customers and to assess their perception of the service you are offering them, you are likely to get a good reading of both their thoughts about you and their emotional responses. When they are unhappy, you will pick up their anger or their criticism directed at you. The most natural responses in these confrontational or tense situations are to try to get them out of your office as quickly as possible, to ignore the problem, or to become confrontational or emotional, as well. Each of these responses puts you in jeopardy of provoking the customer into violence. The alternative is to create win-win situations with irate customers. This requires you to have the ability to stay in control in the situation, get past your own immediate negative reaction to the customer, and find a solution that makes the customer happy, even when she is obnoxious.

The head of an electric utility once said to me, ''We have

customers coming in all the time during this recession complaining about why we are shutting off their electricity due to nonpayment of the bills. Some of them are really irate. We are considering putting in bullet-proof glass throughout our first floor as it is pretty much open to the street. We are also considering bullet-proof glass barriers in our customer service areas. What do you think of doing that?" My response was that it was not a bad idea to put in bullet-proof glass, in spite of the great expense, but that that alone would not be sufficient. A more constructive and effective response to preventing violence in people who were desperately caught between being out of work with no money and having their power shut off was to offer them a resource to help them solve their terribly stressful dilemma. Instead of putting barriers between the utility's customer service people and their customers, could the utility train its employees to maintain their cool in the face of very angry customers? Could it institute a procedure of giving such customers cards with the names, addresses, and phone numbers of the agencies that had the authority to issue temporary funds to help them keep their power on? By providing this service, the utility would be taking a preventive approach to violence by helping the potentially violent individual lower his stress and increasing his ability to cope. The customers could experience the company and its employees as being on their side and as caring about them, rather than as an indifferent enemy. It would also be great value-added customer service.

Generally, measures to prevent violence with customers coincide with the essentials of good customer service. You want to be able to step into the shoes of customers to understand how they experience the situation and what they need from you. If their perception is that they are being shortchanged or taken advantage of, they may choose to retaliate. The individual probably won't be buying from you again, either. Good customer service has to do with listening to your customers because you want to know how they experience your business. You don't want to have former customers floating around feeling wronged by you.

Murder by Current and Former Co-Workers

Larry Hansel had been dismissed from his job as a technician at San Diego's Elgar Corporation. Several months later he returned to the company wearing a bandolier of ammunition around his chest. He shot out the company's telephone network, detonated two radio bombs, and killed two executives. He had no history of violence. Police were called but were given the wrong address. Hansel escaped on bicycle and later turned himself in to the police.

He was a capable technician who had been given repeated warnings about his inappropriate comments at work about religion and politics. He had told a supervisor that he felt additional pressure when required to work overtime. He was known to have a fascination with guns and frequently talked about a shooting spree by a deranged postal worker. He had said that something like the famous Escondido Post Office shootings could happen at Elgar. What he said was not taken as a serious threat.

Later, the company's human resources manager said the incident made him realize the importance of the "soft" side of his role as a senior manager and the need to focus on making the company a more pleasant place to work. The case of Larry Hansel is pretty typical of terminated workers who kill their fellow employees.

In 1992 there was a murder at the Convair Plant of General Dynamics. The facts are as follows:

- Robert Mack was threatened with termination for being late to work twice and absent once.
- He thought he was being sold down the river by the union and by the company.
- The chance of his getting his job back was good, but Mr. Mack didn't believe it.
- He was highly agitated and believed he was going to lose his job.
- During his reinstatement hearing, he shot two executives whom he blamed for his termination, killing his union representative and blinding his supervisor. The warning signs were that his attendance had fallen off and his appearance was a little more disheveled than usual.

In 1993 a young, disgruntled employee who believed that he had been unfairly passed over for a promotion was arrested for the execution-style slaying of two Target department store employees in California's San Gabriel Valley. Sergio Nelson, age 19, with no criminal record, was arrested at home with his grandmother, aunt, and cousin. Robin Shirley and Lee Thompson had been shot with a 9-millimeter handgun as they sat in a car at 4 A.M. waiting for their shift to begin. Shirley had recently received a promotion in the stockroom to a job that Nelson felt he deserved. There had been tension between the two for several weeks. Nelson was reportedly a relatively new employee. The next day co-workers organized a car wash to raise money for the victims' families. Some employees were so distraught that they called in sick. The company sent in a psychologist the next day for any of its 190 employees who might need help and opened a twenty-four-hour phone line for workers.

In September 1989 Joseph Wesbecker, an employee on long-term (mental) disability leave from Standard Gravure Company in Louisville, Kentucky, killed eight co-workers and wounded twelve others with an AK-47 assault rifle. His case illustrates two important aspects of workplace violence: the difficulty of predicting violence and the clear warning signs that assailants often give. Before exploding with violence, Wesbecker had behaved in an increasingly aggressive manner. He had not been confronted early on. His behavior had been ignored. He did not receive the constructive confrontation that is necessary in these situations, and he escalated into violence.

Professor John Monahan has applied his ten risk-assessment questions to this case. These questions can help an observer understand what the potentially violent person is feeling. Let us see what we can learn from the answers:

Q1. *What events precipitated raising the question of the person's potential for violence, and in what context did these events take place?*

A. Wesbecker had voluntarily sought professional help in the past.

Q2. *What are the person's relevant demographic characteristics?*

A. The violent person is typically male, in his late teens or early twenties, of lower socioeconomic status, with a history of substance abuse and frequent job changes, a low IQ, and a poor education. Wesbecker was a male Caucasian, age 47, a high-school dropout who worked for seventeen years at Standard Gravure. He had no history of substance abuse and had an average IQ.

Q3. *What is the person's history of violent behavior?*

A. Neighbors described him as "antisocial, touchy, hotheaded, odd, cranky." He had no known history of violence. A former supervisor said: "You couldn't ask for a better worker."

Q4. *How similar are the past contexts in which the person has used violent coping mechanisms to the contexts in which the person likely will function in the future? Is it possible to reconstruct a pattern of violent behavior?*

A. Wesbecker was away from work on disability for one year without incident. But he did demonstrate an escalating disposition to react to stress with violence.

Q5. *What is the base rate of violent behavior among individuals with this person's background?*

A. There are no base rates of violence in the workplace due to the low frequency of workplace violence.

Q6. *What are the sources of stress in the person's current environment?*

A. Wesbecker complained of chronic toluene exposure on the job. He worked sixteen hours a day, six or seven days a week, so he had no friends. He filed a grievance in October 1986 stating that the company insisted he operate a machine that he found too demanding. In May 1987 he filed a discrimination complaint, and the company then accommodated his mental handicap (manic-depressive illness). The coroner's jury concluded "excessive stress at work was a factor in the murders," even though Wesbecker had not been in the workplace for more than a year prior to the event.

Q7. *What cognitive and emotional factors indicate that the person may be predisposed to cope with stress in a violent manner?* (Cognitive factors determine how people appraise an event and influences whether they respond or not.)

A. Wesbecker had thought and emotional factors that suggested the potential to respond to stress in a violent manner. He was paranoid and wanted revenge. He told a co-worker that he had bought a gun and "would blow his supervisor's brains out" if he said anything to him that didn't pertain directly to work. He made many threats that co-workers failed to take seriously.

Q8. *What cognitive and affective factors indicate that the person may be predisposed to cope with stress in a nonviolent way?*

A. Wesbecker hospitalized himself three times, filed a grievance and a complaint, and sought legal help in an effort to remedy his problems.

Q9. *Who are the likely victims of the person's violence, and how available are they?*

A. Wesbecker encountered no security in entering the plant. No one took the threats seriously. No security was altered.

Q10. *What means does a person possess to commit violence?*

A. Wesbecker owned a pistol and three shotguns, all purchased legally.

Monahan concludes from this case that predicting workplace violence is very complicated. Wesbecker did not demographically fit the profile of a violent person. He had not previously engaged in violent behavior at work. He showed a predisposition to cope with stress in nonviolent ways. Yet he faced considerable stress at work and in his personal life, having had two divorces. In addition, he had thinking and emotional qualities that indicated a potential to react in a violent manner.

This case is typical of people who actually commit workplace murder. Assailants almost always give clear warning signals, but friends and co-workers fail to take the threats seriously. Risk assessments usually must be made with limited information. For example, had the company known of the gun purchases or been informed of the threats verbalized to a friend, Joseph Wesbecker would have been hospitalized involuntarily, and eight people would still be alive.

Threats and Assaults by Current and Former Co-Workers

Unfortunately, there appear to be many employees who act in intimidating ways and make overt threats in the workplace. This can happen while they are on the payroll or, in some cases, after they have left a company's employment. After one of my workplace violence seminars, I received the following letter:

Dear Dr. Labig,

I write to you today with a pleasure of knowing there is something being done about violence in today's workplace. I would like to remain anonymous for reasons of being a victim of a known rapist allowed to retain employment at my previous workplace, who harassed me until my last date of employment. My previous workplace is _____ Corporation, where I held an Automated Systems Tech. position for 5 years.

I was continuously sexually harassed with upper management having knowledge of my complaints. I was pre-warned to leave him alone, of his previous conviction and serving time for raping his own God-daughter, age 12, and of another woman who was also employed at [the company] who is a Spanish-native. She was later terminated after making complaints of this man raping her. From my understandings he served time for this, but was released with a job saved at [the company].

My first complaint took place while expediting paper-work to an isolated office, in the noisy shop on the upper floor of [the building]. I met my harasser with another gentlemen who seemed very nice. As I left a package on a desk, one of the gentlemen left the office. I was then approached by this man making comments as to how pretty and young I was and how he would like to take me to Las Vegas, and how much fun we can have. As I approached the door, with little being said back to him, he put his hand around my waist. I became very afraid, and upset, I told him to stop!! "Get your hands off of me!" He giggled as though it was something cute. He then blocked the office door, with his body.

He wouldn't let me out unless I either kissed him, hugged him, and promised to take off to Las Vegas that coming Friday with him or took his home number in hopes of giving him a positive answer. I was really afraid at this point. I didn't want to agree to any of his propositions, but it was really noisy. If I were to scream, my cries would have never been heard, so I then agreed to take his number but never promised him any-thing. He let me go. Immediately I went into my manager's office with a complaint, but nothing has been resolved. I was asked: "Why was I up there? What did I do to him to trigger this action? Look what you have on." After feeling embar-rassed from this man, of upper position, I went into the em-ployee relations office with hope for help or assistance. I was told by employee relations how much trouble he's caused women in the past in terms of sexual harassment, and his file of serving time for rape, but he (the employee relations) said he couldn't do anything until he spoke with my manager about it. I gave employee relations the telephone number, given to me by this man, as evidence of my complaint to put in my files. . . . From that point on nothing has been resolved, the harassment has continued, from propositions of money to touching and feeling. I began loosing [*sic*] my appetite I was so afraid to go to work, knowing what the day would be like. My parents are aware of this matter and called the [city] Police Department. But they were told nothing could be done because the company is private property, and we would have to go through the company's Investigations Department. We did so; my investigator's first name is Derrick, he tried to help as much as he could but this guy was being saved for unknown reasons. Two weeks into the investigation, I was given a lay-off notice of 60 days so the investigations had to cease. I would no longer be an employee there, but I was still afraid. I also contacted EEO (Equal Employment) downtown for a copy of my file.

My intention in this letter was not to make a short book, but to understand my rights as a citizen. Is there anything else I could have done, if possible, if it isn't too late? If there's anything that your organization can assist me with in this situation, I would really appreciate it. You may contact me by calling _____.

Whatever your reaction to this young woman's letter, it is clear that she is in real distress and in need of assistance and, very likely, protection. At the same time, consider how you would investigate her complaint. How would you distinguish between reality and perception? How would you prove who is telling the truth and who isn't when there are no witnesses? How would you balance each party's rights? These situations can be complicated and sometimes prove to be a legal minefield for the employer who wants to help. As stated in Chapter 1, there is evidence that workplace homicides are only the tip of the iceberg of the violence occurring in companies. What should a company's role be in getting to the heart of situations like this one? How should it respond to her need?

Since starting to try to reverse the rapid increase in the incidence of violence in its facilities, the U.S. Postal Service has found increasing numbers of workers willing to report co-workers who they fear could lose control in a rage. The post office unions are asking for tighter security measures, much as they might have negotiated for better wages and benefits in the past. These requests are not taken as hysteria. Rather, they are seen as an appropriate response to a new level of awareness of the consequences of allowing threats and intimidating behavior to go on uncontrolled within an organization.

Many companies fail to take complaints seriously, and there appears be an overwhelming tendency for most managers to minimize or deny the complaints and fears that employees bring to their attention. Part of the difficulty is that more information is usually needed in order to assess situations like the one described in the letter. There is also a danger that a supervisor may overreact or jump to conclusions. Some work environments become hysterical, and rumors are responded to as if they are facts. The solution to this problem lies in getting to know your employees and having clear procedures for investigating complaints thoroughly.

Domestic Disputes

In April 1993 in Sacramento, California, an accounting supervisor was shot and critically wounded by her former boyfriend in the company's parking lot. Such events are no longer rare exceptions. About twenty women were killed on the job in 1993 by current or former boyfriends or husbands. Domestic disputes have become the third major source of conflict leading to homicide in the workplace. Deterioration of the economy usually brings an increase in domestic violence. The effects of the recession of the early to mid-1990s increasingly are spilling into the workplace as husbands threaten wives at work, where they can locate and confront them. The Justice Department says that in 1993 there were more than 13,000 nonfatal acts of worksite violence committed against women by domestic partners.

Because of the growing volume of domestic violence complaints and years of pressure from women's groups, prosecuting attorneys have begun new strategies for dealing with domestic disputes, including new legal techniques, specially trained prosecution teams, and harsher penalties for violent spouses. Prodded by advocacy groups and publicity from cases in which beatings escalated to murders, prosecutors are hardening their views on domestic crime each year, with some thinking of it as murder prevention. Domestic violence is a crime problem of daunting proportions. The U.S. Surgeon General has identified battering as the country's single largest cause of injury to women. In 1992, 29 percent of all women homicide victims were slain by current or former husbands or boyfriends, according to the FBI.

Part of the problem with domestic violence is something family counselors have known for a long time: There are no simple solutions. It is not clear that counseling is very effective in changing the offender's behavior and in protecting the spouse. Some observers argue that jail sentences are an unrealistic solution. "There simply isn't enough jail space for all the batterers," says University of Maryland criminology professor Lawrence W. Sherman. Morever, he says, "carefully conducted research has yet to be done to determine if jail time really does stop repeat offenses." Sherman, who calls himself a "voice in the wilderness," has equally provocative views on the wisdom of arrests for misdemeanor-level spouse battering. He authored an oft-cited 1983 study that found that arrests did deter repeat offenses, spurring the adoption of state and local mandatory arrest policies. In follow-up studies published in 1992, Sherman and other researchers arrived at much more complex conclusions: Over the long term, the effectiveness of arrest depended on whether the offender was employed. If he was, arrest reduced recidivism. If he was jobless, he was more prone to domestic violence after an arrest.[1]

One question I am always asked at workshops is how to most effectively protect employees who are afraid of a spouse. Sometimes police restraining orders work, and sometimes they make matters worse. Much depends on the willingness of the local police force to enforce them. Many domestic violence cases involve a victim who is struggling emotionally about letting go of the abuser. This can make for a very complex and often frustrating set of problems for co-workers who are trying to be helpful, because all of their suggestions are rejected by the ambivalent or frightened employee who is the potential victim. People often want to retain their privacy at work, but if they are going through

---

[1] "Prosecutors Taking Harder Line Toward Spouse Abuse," *Los Angeles Times* (July 11, 1994).

messy divorces, they need to know that it is all right to let the right persons know at work.

Infatuation and Stalking

A young woman worked with a young man at a blue-collar job. He continued to ask her out in spite of her repeated statements that she wasn't interested. She filed a harassment claim and wrote to the plant manager saying she feared for her safety. The manager did nothing. The man shot and killed the woman and then turned the gun on himself while 125 co-workers watched.

A high-tech executive at a company planning layoffs began to receive threats on electronic mail indicating that she was being observed. As the messages became more graphic and specific in describing her whereabouts accurately, the woman became so terrified she left her job. A year and a half later, she still hadn't returned to work.

In May 1993, thirty-nine-year-old Mark Hilbun shot and knifed his way across Orange County, California. He was later accused of stabbing his sixty-three-year-old mother while she slept, then going to the Dana Point post office and fatally shooting his best friend and wounding a former co-worker. He had become obsessed with a woman co-worker and as a result was fired from the postal job he loved.

A year or more before the shootings, his friends had noticed changes in his behavior. He said he heard voices coming out of his music speakers. He thought the world was coming to an end. He told a friend that when he stabbed his mother, slit the throat of his dog, and shot his best friend, he was convinced he was sparing them from an impending holocaust. He planned to escape into the wild with the woman colleague he was obsessed with and start the human race over again, like Adam and Eve. At times, he also believed himself to be Christ. In April 1993, he had hurled himself from a second-story walkway in an effort to sacrifice himself for mankind.

People who knew him before all this happened described him as quiet. The product of a middle-class home, he had been an average student, mild-tempered and aloof, and he showed little interest in women or sexuality. In March 1990, while a member of the security police squadron at Edwards Air Force Base, he had a psychiatric hospitalization and was diagnosed as having a schizoid personality with depressive features. Apparently he was suicidal at the time. In 1992, a year before the murders, he was seen by those around him as particularly tense and oversensitive. He experienced people as trying to get rid of him.

Suddenly, he became more outgoing, used a lot of profanity, and continually sought out social situations. At that time, he began to harass the woman colleague, who filed a complaint against him with the police. In September he was confronted by his supervisor for playing blaring music from a tape player as he sorted the mail, while singing and dancing and wearing green underwear over his mailman's uniform. His response to the confrontation was to put the underwear on his head. He was escorted out of the office. He returned later to leave his keys, release a white balloon, and leave a baby pacifier for the woman. A co-worker was concerned that he would commit suicide. She called his mother and the postmaster, who alerted the police. Sheriff's deputies took Hilbun from his house to a psychiatric hospital, where he was detained for two weeks. He was diagnosed as having manic-depressive illness and put on medication. Seven months later he calmly walked into the post office with a gun.

Companies cannot afford to trust the institutions of society to care for their employees so that they won't have to give them another thought. Even when a worker is put on disability, medical leave, or terminated, the company has not released itself from liability or protected itself from potential violence. The psychiatric safety net in both the private and the public sectors is now full of holes. A company can best protect itself from the kind of violence Hilbun visited on his organization by realizing that providing support and mental health services and maintaining supportive relationships with estranged or even terminated employees may be in the company's best interest. Some form of careful monitoring and limited but continual communication with those individuals who have sent clear warning signs of grievances or potential targets at work is a good investment.

Remember the case of Mark Hilbun when you have an employee on leave or termination status and are considering extending health care benefits for hospitalization, providing counseling services through an employee assistance program, or simply having a former manager or a human resources professional maintain a caring, supportive relationship with the person.

Chapter 4

Can I Keep the Violent Out by Not Hiring Them?

We are unable to predict with certainty who will eventually become violent. However, we know enough about the spiral of violence to identify the characteristics, emotional responses, and ways of thinking that make a person more likely to use violence when under severe stress and when circumstances permit. We can use this knowledge to assess an employee's potential for acting violently at five points in the employment process:

1. *During the hiring process,* when an applicant can be examined and any indications of heightened risk of violent behavior can be pursued (this is the subject of this chapter).
2. *When it spills into the workplace,* as in a conflict with a customer or when a family member with whom the employee is having a problem shows up at the worksite (see Chapter 3).
3. *When major changes are being made in the workplace,* e.g., downsizing or significant work reassignments (see Chapter 6 and Chapter 9).
4. *During ongoing counseling of a troubled employee,* when the employee may reveal information that suggests that violent behavior is imminent or that a crisis is occurring or about to occur (see Chapter 7).
5. *During the course of employment,* when a supervisor may refer an employee to an occupational health physician or

to an employee assistance program or when an employee refers herself at a point when she fears a loss of control (see Chapter 7).

The best time to assess an employee's potential for acting violently is during the hiring process. Screening for hiring offers a natural opportunity to evaluate a person's likelihood of becoming violent later on the job.

Some employers have attempted to use preemployment screening procedures to identify employment candidates who have a predisposition toward or a history of violent conduct. For many companies, this means applying a "profile" to applicants. Screening would be easier if the violent employee fit a narrow definition (e.g., male, white, 35–50 years of age, closely identified with his job, and with multiple outside pressures, such as marital problems). Unfortunately, this describes a large percentage of employees. In order to screen out applicants fitting this profile, employers would have to eliminate a large percentage of their qualified applicant pool, in addition to many of their current employees.

Using Psychological Testing as a Predictor of Violence

Given what we know about the emergence of violent behavior, no psychological tests can sufficiently measure a person's circumstances, responses, and internal thoughts and feelings to make an accurate prediction about how the person will behave. Claims to the contrary are dangerous because they can lead a company into a false sense of security, a belief that it has taken care of its risk dangers when in reality it has not. The effectiveness of psychological tests in screening out individuals with the capacity to commit acts of violence has never been proved.

The use of psychological testing in employment decisions is under attack in the courts. Many pre-offer applicant screening tests have been rendered illegal by the Americans with Disabilities Act (ADA), which outlaws employment discrimination against qualified individuals with disabilities, including mental illness, and prohibits the use of medical examinations on applicants prior to a job offer. Although the ADA does not specifically include psychological tests in this prohibition, it can be assumed that psychological tests will be treated as medical exams. Employers may make a job offer conditional on the satisfactory result of a post-offer medical exam or medical inquiry if the exam is required of all entering employees in the same job category. Any decision to revoke a job offer for an applicant on the basis of failure to pass a medical exam must be job-related and based on business necessity.

The ADA allows employers to refuse employment to a person if a post-offer psychological test or evaluation establishes that he poses a "direct threat" to the health or safety of himself or others. In that case, the employer must meet very specific requirements in order to establish that a "direct threat" exists. Practically speaking, the company cannot rely solely on existing psychological tests, because the value of current tests in predicting violence is very uncertain. A conclusion that a person has tendencies to be violent is not sufficient under the direct-threat standard of ADA to exclude a candidate who can later claim a mental disability. The ADA does not require that you hire or retain someone who is making a direct threat to the health or safety of himself or a co-worker if there is a real and specific threat and a high probability that severe harm will occur. You are allowed to ask questions to clarify any of these issues.

In short, employers cannot use general psychological tests for applicants before making a job offer and essentially cannot use the results of such tests to revoke a job offer. The results of such tests are not by themselves, in most cases, sufficient to meet the strict standards required to establish that an employee is a direct threat.

Some states have also banned the use of psychological screening tests because they are seen as an invasion of applicants' right to privacy. To be legal, tests must directly relate to the job for which the person is applying. Both federal law and some state laws prohibit the compulsory use of lie detector tests for applicants, making polygraph testing unavailable as a means of screening out potentially violent applicants.

If psychological testing and polygraph tests are invalid and illegal, then what means can employers use to determine if applicants have a propensity toward violence? Selection interviews, including psychological interviews, and reference checks are the only acceptable methods for getting at a candidate's risk for violence on the job.

Let us turn our attention to how to conduct such interviews in a way that gets at risk of future violence but complies with the ADA and other federal regulations.

Interviewing to Assess Risk of Violence

Many of the questions that should be asked of a job applicant in a good interview get at the issues of risk and are perfectly legal and appropriate. The best way to approach this issue is to define the essential characteristics of success in the position under question and to develop good questions to measure the candidate's ability in those areas. Increasingly, companies are finding that human relations skills are as important as technical skills in job success at all levels. Listing and defining those skills in job descriptions and questioning the applicant's approach and style in those areas will serve double duty, predicting both job success and violence potential.

Questions must be job-related. Thus, you can't ask the person if she suffers from a mental illness, because if it is kept under control with medication, the illness will probably not create a problem for job performance or violence. Further, mental illness can qualify as a disability under the ADA, so you are not allowed to ask general or vague questions about it.

Think back to John Monahan's model for predicting violence, described in Chapter 2. Predicting violence requires an understanding of the subjective or internal experience a person is having, including his cognitive and emotional processes, such as predisposing and inhibiting appraisals and expectations, predisposing and inhibiting emotional reactions, behavioral coping skills, and general life situation. By asking questions and listening as candidates describe themselves and their behaviors in each of these areas, you will learn a lot about how they will act and how they will deal with different situations on the job. Their answers are usually relevant to predicting their success on the job, whether you are interviewing them for a sales position and want to know how they will deal with customers or for an executive role, where managing and motivating other people will be critical. Asking individuals to describe themselves and understanding how they really see themselves helps get at these issues.

A key component of cognitive or thought processes is expectations. If I think that I have to act in a certain way to accomplish my goals, that is how I will act. These beliefs can be surfaced by asking the person about situations in which there was conflict or in which she had difficulty accomplishing a goal. Besides learning what the person did in those situations, you want to understand how she thought about them. What would she do differently if she were to face the same situation again? What does she typically do to accomplish her goals? People who become violent on the job typically do not see any other options for resolving problems. How does the candidate solve problems? Is she able to come up with constructive solutions for conflict, or are problems seen as other people's fault? Does the applicant take responsibility for her shortcomings?

To assess the individual's predisposing or inhibiting emotional responses, you need to have her explain how she felt in different situations of conflict or stress. How does she express anger? How does she feel when faced with the pressure of many demands at work? To what degree do her various emotional and cognitive reactions lead to decisions about how to handle a situation? Is she able to describe genuinely empathic feelings for what other people go through? Is there an appreciation for the consequences that one's own actions have other people? Finally, you want to get a sense of how she deals with stress in her life. People often describe themselves and their circumstances if given the opportunity in an interview. An interviewer can often form an accurate impression of the supports a person may have in her life and of her ability to use these supports in times of stress. An isolated person who must rely on his own internal resources is more vulnerable to feeling overwhelmed and desperate than someone who is comfortable reaching out to available friends, family, or professionals for help in solving problems and in dealing with provocative feelings.

Good interviews are not inquisitions. Interviewers should spend little time talking and the majority of the time listening. A few well-positioned questions let the candidate share who he is without having his privacy invaded or fielding embarrassing questions. Every company that interviews applicants should have someone designated to have this kind of "get-acquainted" conversation. It should be relaxed and comfortable, not pressured, and designed to get to know what the person is really like. Does he turn to alcohol to cope? Does she have severe depressions? Has she learned from the problems she has faced in life, or is she bitter and defensive? Is his tendency to strike out or to turn inward? All of these questions may be answered without the interviewer's ever asking them, simply by spending time getting to know the applicant.

Many companies have turned to candidate evaluations by corporate psychologists to assess an applicant's "fit" to a job and to a company. These evaluations are legal and useful if they focus on understanding the person in terms of the criteria for success in the job. Simply looking at a candidate's personality is not relevant and is legally questionable. However, assessing an individual's characteristics, skills, and abilities as they compare with the critical success factors for a given position is very useful. Such evaluations help avoid costly hiring mistakes and provide the side benefit of screening for violence potential by measuring the interpersonal skills, cognitive and emotional style, behavioral history, and coping strategies of the individual. I have done hundreds of candidate assessments over the years, and they can provide an accurate basis for distinguishing many of the elements related to a person's likelihood of becoming violent on the job. To the degree that a company defines human relations abilities as part of its success criteria, all of these factors become immediately job-related. In fact, they surface the major derailment issues that most commonly create failure on the job over time.

Performing Reference Checks

Besides interviewing, the most common form of screening job applicants is preemployment background checks through various external sources. Relevant information can be gathered through the Department of Motor Vehicles about the applicant's driving record and through civil, bankruptcy, divorce, and criminal court filings. Most court records are available to the public and provide a wealth of information. Most companies want to screen out applicants who have a history of legal convictions or of any violent behavior. There is some justification for these exclusions, because people who have been violent are probably more likely to be violent again. Of course, many instances of workplace violence are caused by people with no history of violence.

During pre-employment interviews, you may ask a candidate about any prior criminal convictions but not about arrests that did not lead to conviction. Some states also allow inquiries about arrests for molestation if the individual is applying for a child-care job or about drugs if the individual is applying for a job that involves handling pharmaceuticals.

The courts are increasingly placing blame on companies for hiring a person with a criminal record if he later commits an act of violence against a fellow employee or customer. Courts are finding the employer negligent in hiring or retaining such an individual. In *Yunker v. Honeywell,* an employer in Minnesota was held liable in 1993 for negligent supervision, retention, and hiring of an employee with a manslaughter conviction who made death threats and then murdered a co-worker while off duty. In 1990 an employer was found liable for hiring and failing to supervise a prior offender from a rehabilitation program who beat a customer.

This does not mean that employers must automatically exclude all applicants with criminal records from employment. Some state laws even prohibit the exclusion of applicants for government jobs solely on the basis of a prior criminal conviction. Even if an employee with a criminal record commits an act of violence against a co-worker or customer, the employer is not ordinarily held liable unless the attack was reasonably foreseeable and the employer ignored warning signs, such as threats. Employers should therefore attempt to get as much information as possible about the circumstances of any prior convictions from the applicant and from the authorities and then analyze whether the applicant can reasonably be placed in a particular job without significant fear of misconduct or violence. An applicant who has been convicted of felony assault on a woman, for example, should not be hired by a hospital as a night-shift technician where he will come into contact with a large number of women patients and employees while under little supervision. On the other hand, if that same individual applies for a position as file clerk where he will come into contact with women only on rare occasions and only while being supervised, then he should not automatically be rejected. A pre-employment background check may reduce the risk of a negligence suit later by an injured co-worker or customer or by members of a victim's family. But it may also bring about discrimination suits by rejected applicants under discrimination laws or common-law notions such as invasion of privacy.

The other screening mechanism that employers commonly use for job applicants is an intensive background check with prior employers. Many former employers are reluctant to provide negative information for fear of being sued for defamation, so many provide only neutral data about employees, such as dates of employment. In spite of this, most managers still attempt to talk with former employers about an applicant's work record. Obviously, the circumstances under which an applicant left former employers may reveal a lot about his history of conflict, threats, or violence. A thorough background check on an applicant's employment history, including conviction information and contact with former employers, can often help a company avoid liability if an employee later commits a violent act in the workplace. Employers should also be sure to state on their application that applicants who make false statements on their applications can and will be rejected or, if the falsehood is discovered after hire, terminated. Such a policy gives an employer a solid basis upon which to reject or terminate an individual if the employer learns, for example, of a prior conviction during a background check and the applicant has stated on the application that he has no criminal record.

Making Hiring Decisions

Many companies are deciding that, in the face of intense competition, they can no longer afford to hire people who are mediocre performers or who are likely to fail on the job. They are therefore putting increased energy and focus into hiring decisions. A company can protect itself from the dual perils of making a costly error in selection and of hiring someone who is likely to become violent if it defines the critical factors for job success in terms of both technical skills and the human relations skills. These traits and skills should be consistent with the organization's rules of behavior and culture.

In a high-performance environment, no matter how skilled the applicant, she must also possess a basic ability to be a team player. Over and over, hiring managers are seduced away from this basic principle. In most cases, assessing the human relations skills that foster success with customers or co-workers also enables interviewers to evaluate risk factors for workplace violence. People with low tolerance for frustration, little empathy, a habit of blaming others when there are problems, and a bias toward striking out when tensions rise are poor risks in terms of not only potential violence but effective job performance. Looked at this way, a focus on violence prevention in hiring directly supports the success of the business. On the other hand, if your company has a highly pressured, sadistic culture, you need to hire people who can cope in such an atmosphere while maintaining adequate self-control.

The other tack that a company can take to protect itself is to get to know prospective employees well before making a final decision about hiring. Even in this case, however, there are no guarantees that a company will avoid hiring someone with the potential to become violent. Many types of people can become violent under the right circumstances. Nonetheless, if the interviewer spends enough time listening, there is a chance that some indicators of the likelihood of violence will surface. At the very least, the company will gain a better understanding of the strengths and weaknesses of candidates, putting it in a much better position to deal with a crisis later on, should one occur. This is especially true if there has been proper documentation along the way of problems in work performance or interpersonal adjustment.

Chapter 5

Legal and Liability Issues

Garry Mathiason, Sim Avila, and Deanna Mouser
Littler, Mendelson, Fastiff, Tichy, and Mathiason

This chapter discusses the legal issues surrounding workplace violence and provides guidance regarding the often conflicting rights of the victim, the perpetrator, and third parties. In addition, it describes the close attention that courts are now giving to workplace violence and the scores of legislative efforts currently under way across the United States to deal with it.[1]

Employers' Duties and Legal Obligations to Employees

Occupational Safety and Health Requirements

The federal Occupation Safety and Health Act (Fed-OSH Act) and its state counterparts generally require employers to provide

[1] The law with respect to liability of employers for violence in the workplace is still evolving. While many legal theories discussed in this chapter are established precedent, some sources of liability discussed are potential extensions of existing law. The discussion of such possible extensions of the law should not be taken as a prediction of future developments. They are included simply to aid employers to avoid potential claims.

their employees with a place of employment that is "free from recognized hazards that are causing or are likely to cause death or serious physical harm to ... employees."[2] Encompassed within this general requirement is the obligation to do everything reasonably necessary to protect employees' life, safety, and health, including furnishing safety devices and safeguards and adopting practices reasonably adequate to create a safe and healthful workplace.

Employers who learn of threats of violence against the employees or who know that the risk of violence is high may be required under the Fed-OSH Act to take action to prevent injury or protect employees if violence erupts. Indeed, the federal Occupational Safety and Health Administration (OSHA) has issued a significant number of citations that are intended to encourage employers to take affirmative steps to prevent employees' injuries. OSHA has instructed its inspectors to use the general provisions of Section 654(a)(1) of the California Labor Code to cite workplaces where criminal activity endangers workers.

Both federal and state OSHA agencies are actively studying workplace violence and are likely to promulgate regulations directing employers to take steps to diminish the possibility of workplace violence. Indeed, California OSHA has already done so. On August 15, 1994, Cal-OSHA's Division of Occupational Safety and Health promulgated new guidelines for workplace security. These guidelines require employers to adopt a written plan to prevent workplace violence.

The best way to avoid liability under such acts is to address workplace security issues and to provide training concerning violent situations as part of the employer's safety program.

Negligent Hiring, Training, Supervision, and Retention of Employees

An employer may be liable for carelessness in hiring, training, supervision, and retention of employees. It has a duty to protect its employees and customers for injuries caused by employees who the employer knows, or should know, pose a risk of harm to

[2] 29 USC § 654(a)(1); *see also* Cal. Lab. Code § 6400.

others. The duty is breached when an employer fails to exercise reasonable care to ensure that its employees and customers are free from risk of harm.

Many state courts have recognized that employers have a duty to investigate their applicants' backgrounds to prevent the risk of violent acts directed at employees and others. In New Mexico, a court determined that an employer was liable for negligently hiring a doorman who assaulted a patron. The employer knew that the doorman previously had been involved in fights at the employer's bar and elsewhere and posed a danger to patrons. The court held that the employer knew, or should have known, that the doorman was unsuitable for employment in view of the risk he posed to others.

Employers can take several steps to protect themselves against liability for negligent hiring. For example:

1. Carefully review all information on employment applications and resumés before hiring an applicant, and question the applicant about any gaps in his employment history. Such gaps could be a result of serving time for violent crimes.[3]

2. Contact each prior employer to verify dates of employment and positions held, and try to determine the applicant's reliability, honesty, and tendency toward violence. These efforts should all be documented, even if they are unsuccessful, and the employer should not make an offer of employment until the screening process has been completed.

3. Advise the applicant that omissions, misrepresentation, or falsification of information will result in rejection of the applicant or in termination of employment.

Courts have also held the employer liable when one employee asserts that the employer should have taken reasonable care in supervising a second employee who is threatening the first employee with violent conduct. The Supreme Court of South

---

[3] Federal and state laws severely restrict preemployment inquiries, investigations, and testing. Furthermore, the investigations into the use of prior criminal records in hiring decisions is often strictly limited. Legal counsel should therefore be consulted.

Carolina ruled in 1992 that an employer may be liable for negligent supervision if the employee intentionally harms another person while on the employer's property or while using the employer's equipment, if the employer knows or should know that the employer has the ability to control the employee and if the employer knows or should know of the necessity for exercising such control.

An employer that does not recognize an applicant's violent tendencies at the time of hiring despite having followed steps intended to prevent negligent hiring claims, must still take steps to prevent workplace violence. In a Minnesota case, a company had employed a violent employee for two years and then reemployed him after he had been imprisoned for five years for the strangulation death of a co-worker. He was rehired as a custodian and transferred twice because of workplace confrontations. He then shot and killed another co-worker. The Minnesota Court of Appeals concluded that the trustee of the estate of the latest victim did not have a claim for negligent hiring or supervision but did have a claim for negligent retention. The court reasoned that the employer should have realized that the employee posed a danger to co-workers but failed to take preventive action, such as investigating, discharging, or reassigning the employee. Because the risk was foreseeable, the employer had a duty of care that was not outweighed by the policy consideration of providing employment opportunities for former felons.

To avoid negligent retention suits, the employer must take remedial action to separate a violent employee from other employees and customers. The employer should consider suspending the employee pending a thorough investigation of allegations of violence and should expressly prohibit the employee from returning to the workplace until the investigation is completed. The employer may need to enforce this, e.g., by increasing security measures or by retrieving the employee's key access card.

Statutory Duties to Train Employees
to Avoid Violence

Responding to the threat of workplace violence, the California legislature enacted in 1993 a new law that requires specified hospitals to conduct security and safety assessments, develop a security plan, and train specified employees by July 1, 1995.

Employees regularly assigned to the emergency department must be trained on a continuing basis on the following topics:

- General safety measures
- Personal safety measures
- The assault cycle
- Aggression- and violence-predicting factors
- How to obtain patient history from a patient with violent behavior
- Characteristics of aggressive and violent patients and victims
- Verbal and physical maneuvers to defuse and avoid violent behavior
- Strategies for avoiding physical harm
- Restraining techniques
- Appropriate use of medications as chemical restraints
- Any resources available to employees for coping with incidents of violence (e.g., critical incident stress debriefing and employee assistance programs)

It appears to be only a matter of time before other employers will be required to provide similar training to their employees to prevent violent incidents and to minimize the severity and frequency of injuries when violence does erupt. Cal-OSHA has already announced its intent to move in this direction by making prevention and training a responsibility for California employers.

Contracts and Implied Obligations

Employers may have other obligations to employees stemming from employment contracts and implied agreements. Contractual obligations can arise without written or express agreements. For example, the California Supreme Court ruled that an implied contract may be inferred from the language in a company's policy manual or employee handbook.[4] Employees or third parties

---

[4] *Foley v. Interactive Data Corp.*, 47 Cal. 3d 654 (1988).

can use company policies on workplace safety as the basis of a suit against the company for violating an implied contract.

Employers may also have duties to their employees resulting from the implied covenant of good faith and fair dealing, which holds that neither party can act in bad faith to deprive the other of contractual benefits. The covenant requires the parties to be fair with one another in applying contract terms. Thus, it could be argued that by signing an employment agreement, an employer agrees to provide a safe working environment that enables employees to perform their jobs.

Obligations Stemming From Public Policy

An employee who complains about unsafe working conditions or who refuses to work in an unsafe work environment and is terminated may be able to sue the employer for wrongful termination in violation of public policy. Several states have awarded damages to terminated employees from their employer, even though the employer had the right to fire the employee, if the termination violated fundamental principles of public policy.

In a Maryland case, a teacher at a private residential and educational facility for troubled adolescent females was fired, allegedly for notifying state authorities about the danger posed to staff and residents by "gangs" at the facility. The court ruled that she had a claim for wrongful discharge in violation of public policy, which required that suspected child abuse and neglect be reported.

Other legal obligations can be attributed to employers on the basis of special duties imposed upon the employees themselves. One is a judicially created duty based on a California finding that a therapist must at least warn an intended victim if one of the therapist's patients poses a severe danger to that person. By extension, employers also have broad duties and responsibilities not only to employees but to third parties, whether they grow out of the law, contracts, or other legal bases.

Duty to Warn Targeted Victims

It is probably just a matter of time before courts recognize an employer's duty to warn targeted victims of workplace violence.

The courts may reach this conclusion on the basis of judicially created public policy, such as the California decision just discussed. As courts around the nation increasingly impose liability for negligence in hiring and retaining employees who terrorize workplaces by violent acts, courts may also use the same reasoning to impose liability on employers for negligent failure to warn the targeted victim.

Courts may base the duty to warn employees of work-related violence on occupational safety and health laws, especially in view of OSHA's recent announcement of its intent to include issues of criminal activity that endangers workers in its definition of an employer's obligation to provide a safe workplace. California corporations and managers already face criminal liability for failing to disclose concealed hazards for which there is a substantial probability of death, great bodily harm, or serious exposure.

Foreseeability is the key component for establishing liability. Even though determining the question of whether an employer owes a duty to an employee must be decided on a case-by-case basis, the California Supreme Court has ruled that "every case is governed by the rule of general application that all persons are required to use ordinary care to prevent others from being injured as the result of their conduct."[5]

It is highly probable that once a court must decide where an employer has a duty to take precautionary measures to protect employees from workplace violence, the court will conclude that such a duty exists. However, it is also probable that the court will consider the cost of precautionary measures when determining the scope of the employer's obligation. For example, a California court noted that because of the substantial monetary cost incurred, the hiring of security guards will rarely be justified in the absence of prior similar incidents of violent crime on the premises.

Rights of the Alleged Perpetrator

Defamation Claims

An employer who mistakenly believes that someone has violent tendencies and who then warns employees about that person

---

[5] *J'Aire Corp. v. Gregory*, 24 Cal 3d 799, 780 (1979).

can be found liable for defamation. (Defamation occurs when a statement that is communicated to another individual is false, unprivileged, and the cause of injury.[6]) Regardless of whether the statement is verbal (slander) or written (libel), the employer can be held liable for a false characterization that an employee is violent.

An employer who is mistaken in telling other employees that an individual has violent tendencies may be protected because the warning was privileged. A qualified privilege applies if the employer had a good-faith belief in the statement's truth, the statement served a legitimate business interest, and the information was given only to those with the need to know of the risk. Thus, when the employer believes in good faith that an employee has engaged in violent behavior and warns that person's co-workers of this to protect them, a qualified privilege should apply to the employer's warning even if the employee is later found not to have violent tendencies.

To establish a basis for proving the requisite good-faith belief, the employer should conduct a prompt investigation of the allegations of violence or threats *before* warning others. This is crucial if the employer merely hears a rumor that an employee has engaged in violent conduct and the source of the rumor is not willing to substantiate it. An employer abuses its qualified privilege when it fails to investigate statements that lack basic credibility.

Wrongful Discharge Claims

An employee who is accused of having violent tendencies and is terminated for that reason may file a wrongful discharge suit against the employer if the employee disputes the employer's characterization and the decision to terminate the employee.

An employer should take steps to minimize both the threat of violence and the risk of a wrongful discharge suit or grievance.

---

[6] For further background, see W. Prosser and W. Keeton, *Prosser and Keeton on the Law of Torts*, 5th ed. (West, 1984), pp. 773–778.

Before a threat or actual act of violence even occurs, the employer should review its employee handbook and personnel policies to ensure that they contain no statements that could be interpreted as creating an implied contract that could keep the employer from immediately terminating a violent employee. For example, the highest court in West Virginia rejected an employee's claim, based on the employment manual, of wrongful discharge. The court pointed out that the manual provided for immediate discharge for fighting or engaging in any activity that may result in bodily injury to employees or guests.

After an allegation that a threat or actual act of violence occurred, an employer can consider suspending the alleged perpetrator while investigating the allegation to determine if the allegations have merit. This could serve the goals of preventing workplace violence and avoiding a wrongful discharge suit should the violence allegations turn out to be a hoax or otherwise unsubstantiated. An employer might also consider encouraging a resignation if this alternative would ease tension and the risk of violence.

Invasion of Privacy Claims

The protection of privacy rights arises from federal and state constitutions as well as from court-developed law. Although an employer has an obligation to investigate any threats of workplace violence to safeguard other employees and customers, the employer must ensure that it conducts its investigation legally and as unobtrusively as possible.

In addition to a constitutional claim, an employee may file a tort action for invasion of privacy. One type of privacy tort involves an intrusion of solitude or an intrusion into private affairs.[7] The employee who files such a claim must establish intentional intrusion, physically or otherwise, on the employee's solitude or into the employee's private affairs and that the intrusion would be highly offensive to a reasonable person, whether or not the employer does not actually uncover any embarrassing or private information.

[7] See *Prosser and Keeton,* pp. 854–856.

A second invasion of privacy tort is the public disclosure of private facts where that disclosure is offensive and objectionable to a reasonable person and the facts are not of legitimate public concern.[8] Even though all of the information revealed is true, this tort may still be established because its basis is the public disclosure to a large audience. Where the employer has a legitimate reason for the disclosure, such as employee safety, the facts are of legitimate public concern and there should be no liability for warning others.

A third privacy tort can be established when the employee is presented in a false light to the public and a reasonable person would find such public disclosure offensive.[9] Where the warnings of violent tendencies are based on objective and verified facts, the employer should again not be liable, because the employer has not placed the perpetrator in a false light.

Interference With Economic Interests

If a third party insists that an employer fire an employee believed to have violent propensities, the employee may be able to establish a claim against that third party.

California and other state courts have recognized the tort of negligent interference with prospective economic advantage. However, it may be difficult for an employee accused of workplace violence to establish that the third party owes the employee a duty of care.

Some jurisdictions recognize the affirmative defense of justification to defeat a claim of interference with economic interests. A defendant who uses lawful means to induce an employer to breach a contract is justified, and therefore privileged, if his objectives in doing so are more important than the losses suffered by the employee. If the third party is interfering with the employee's employment to protect an individual's safety and not with

[8] See *Prosser and Keeton,* pp. 856–863.
[9] See *Prosser and Keeton,* pp. 863–866.

an improper intent, a court is likely to conclude that the interference was justified.

Discrimination Under the Americans with Disabilities Act

The Americans with Disabilities Act (ADA) and related state statutes prohibit employers from discriminating against "qualified individuals" with physical or mental disabilities. An employer confronted with workplace violence must examine the perpetrator's legal rights and the employer's obligations to other employees. What if the employee who is alleged to have committed a violent act then claims that his behavior is the result of a mental impairment or disability and requests an accommodation for that disability? Must the employer consider the request? And what would a reasonable accommodation be?

These questions were addressed specifically by the Florida courts. A terminated employee alleged that he was discriminated against under the ADA when he was discharged for unauthorized possession of a firearm. The employee claimed that he had a chemical imbalance and that he was therefore a "qualified individual with a disability" under the ADA. He also claimed that this chemical imbalance caused him to carry the firearm on the defendant's property. The court decided that the employee did have a chemical imbalance that qualified as a disability, as claimed, and that the employer was required to make a reasonable accommodation if the plaintiff could perform the essential functions of his job.

This case illustrates the complex problems that must be addressed in situations implicating the provisions of the ADA and argues for cooperation between an employer's human resources department, labor counsel, and occupational physicians. Employers must consider the legal obligations to both the threatening employee and the intended target employees. Furthermore, although under the ADA a temporary impairment that affects a major life activity may or may not be classified as a disability, an employer must be cautioned not to base its decision on whether a disability is covered by the Act on generalities, preconceptions, or groundless fears. There is a need for thorough assessment and consideration of all the circumstances to determine whether the person is a "qualified individual" with a disability and whether a reasonable accommodation can or should be made in each instance.

Employers' Liabilities Under Workers' Compensation

Employers' Liabilities: The California Model

The role of the workers' compensation system is significant in workplace violence but varies from state to state. For this discussion, the California model is used. In many states, including California, in order for an injury to be compensable under the workers' compensation statutes, an employee's injury must not only be sustained in the course of employment (during the performance of service) but must arise out of the employment. If these requirements are met, with a few exceptions, the workers' compensation system generally provides the only recourse, and workers are precluded from seeking other civil claims against the employer.

Workplace Assaults

A workplace assault is compensable under the workers' compensation laws if the subject matter of the dispute leading to the assault involves the work itself or the work brought the injured employee and the perpetrator together and created the conditions and relations that resulted in the altercation.

Injuries resulting from personal disputes in the workplace are often held compensable because, as the court found in one California case, "work places [people] under strains and fatigue from human and mechanical impacts, creating frictions which explode in myriads of ways." Although injuries resulting from purely personal animosity unconnected to employment are generally not compensable, injuries are compensable if the employment increases or contributes to the risk of the assault.

A workplace assault that is purely personal and unrelated to the employment is not compensable under workers' compensation. Injuries are not deemed to have arisen out of the employment where the following conditions are present:

- The employee's duties do not place the employee in a position of particular danger, or the risk of harm is not limited to the place of employment.
- The assault occurs on the employer's premises while the victim was on the premises but was not performing duties of employment at the time of the assault.
- The nature of the employment was not part of the assailant's plan to isolate or trap the employee.

Assaults by spouses or significant others generally are personally motivated and fit into the category of noncompensable injuries under the Workers' Compensation Act. For example, injuries a bartender sustained when the jealous husband of a cocktail waitress assaulted him were not covered under workers' compensation, as the assault was personal and did not arise out of the employment; the bartender's place of employment did not make him particularly susceptible to such injuries.

However, an employee shot by her former husband was held to be covered by workers' compensation where the victim's employment contributed to the injury. The employee worked for a company that made table pads, and her job involved going to customers' apartments to measure their tables. The employee's former husband placed an order to get her to come to an apartment that he had rented. When she arrived, he shot her and killed himself. The court held that the woman's employment contributed to her death by placing her in an isolated location where her former husband could implement his plan.

A husband's shooting of his wife at her place of employment

was covered under workers' compensation where the husband had made repeated threats, including telling his wife's employer of his specific intent to kill his wife at work on a particular day. The employer knew the precise day and place that the husband planned to carry out his scheme and not only failed to warn the employee but refused her repeated requests for a transfer. The court held that according to the husband's threat, the risk of harm was limited to the grocery store where the wife worked. Therefore, there was a special risk in her place of employment, and her injuries were covered under workers' compensation.

In the absence of such special exposure or special circumstances, third-party assaults against employees are generally not covered under workers' compensation unless the assailant intends to injure the employer by committing a violent act against the employer's employee. For example, the rape of a flight attendant while she was on a layover between flights was not covered under workers' compensation because there was no evidence that the assailant intended to harm Western Airlines through the rape of its employee.[10]

Psychological Injuries

Some states continue to restrict an employee's ability to receive workers' compensation benefits for psychological injuries unless the employment contributed significantly to the psychiatric problem. For example, California law requires an employee to demonstrate by a preponderance of the evidence that the actual events of employment were "predominant" among all of the combined causes for the psychiatric injury. However, an employee whose psychological injury has resulted from "being a victim of a violent act of from direct exposure to a significant violent act" need only establish by a preponderance of the evidence that actual events of employment were a "substantial

[10] *Western Airlines v. Workers' Compensation Appeals Board*, 155 Cal. App. 3d 366 (1984).

cause" of the injury, which means at least 35 to 40 percent of the cause was due to the actual events of employment.

Employer's Willful or Serious Misconduct

The workers' compensation system generally provides the exclusive remedy for employee injuries sustained during the employment relationship, and the worker will be precluded from seeking other civil claims against the employer. However, an employer's willful or serious misconduct towards an employee constitutes a startling exception to this general exclusivity rule. A California court has held that an employer's willful attack on an employee is not a risk or a condition of employment. Accordingly, an injury resulting from an employer's intentional assault on an employee is compensable under workers' compensation and may also be the subject of a civil action for damages. In such a case, the remedies may be cumulative rather than mutually exclusive. Thus, a worker who was threatened by a supervisory employee with a gun at the place of employment was allowed to bring a tort suit against his employer. Furthermore, where an employee acts as the employer's agent in harming another employee, the employer can be liable for damages in a civil action.

An employer can be liable to an employee for increased compensation in the amount of one-half of the workers; compensation award where the employee is injured by reason of the employer's serious and willful misconduct. This liability is not insurable. An employer commits willful misconduct when it deliberately fails to act for its employees safety, knowing that this failure will probably result in injury to them. For example, a parking lot attendant was awarded increased benefits for injuries sustained from a beating during robbery where the employer knew of a previous robbery attempt and previous robberies in nearby garages and yet failed to provide a cash register and took no other action to direct robbers away from the employee but rather required the employee to keep the cash on his person.

Workers' Compensation and the Perpetrator

An employee who commits a violent act in the workplace and who sustains injury during the course of a violent act may or may not be entitled to workers' compensation benefits. California workers' compensation law bars recovery of benefits in the following circumstances:

- Where the injury is intentionally self-inflicted
- Where the employee willfully and deliberately causes his or her own death
- Where the injury arises out of an altercation in which the employee is the initial physical aggressor
- Where the injury is caused by the commission of a felonious act or certain other specified crimes

These exceptions are likely to prevent the perpetrator of a violent act in the workplace from recovering workers' compensation benefits for injuries sustained during the course of the violent act.

This rule, however, is misleading and does not preclude workers' compensation coverage to every employee who commits a violent act in the workplace. It applies only if an injury arises out of the altercation and if the injured employee is *the initial physical aggressor.*

Determining whether the employee was the initial physical aggressor is difficult. The initial physical aggressor is not necessarily the person who makes the first physical contact. The initial physical aggressor is the employee who approaches a fellow worker in such a manner that the co-worker has reason to fear bodily harm, even though the employee does not actually attempt to hurt him.

Prevention and the Special Role of the Criminal Justice System

To prevent workplace violence, an employer may be able to encourage local law enforcement officials to pursue criminal law sanctions against an individual, especially if that person is a former employee or a third party. Although local law enforcement officials will be familiar with the possible criminal laws on which to rely, employers may want to be aware of the basic criminal statutes that may be applied to a perpetrator of workplace violence. For example:

• *Antistalking laws.* As a result of numerous incidents in which individuals obsessively follow, harass, or kill others, most states have enacted laws that prohibit "stalking" or harassment. California, for example, enacted such a law after the harassment and death of the actress Rebecca Schaeffer.

In California, it is now a misdemeanor for any person to willfully, maliciously, and repeatedly follow or harass another and to make a credible threat with intent to place that person in reasonable fear for his or her safety or the safety of his or her immediate family. The California Penal Code likewise provides penalties for violating a temporary restraining order that prohibits such stalking (and, presumably, a temporary restraining order prohibiting civil harassment). A repeat offender of California's antistalking law is subject to progressively greater criminal penalties.

• *Threatening or annoying telephone calls.* California Penal Code Section 653(m)(c) prohibits repeated telephone calls made to a person at a place of work with an intent to annoy that person if:

1. There is a temporary restraining order, an injunction, or any other court order in effect prohibiting this behavior and/or
2. The person makes more than ten such calls in a twenty-four-hour period to a person at her place of work with an intent to annoy that person when that person is a spouse, former spouse, cohabitant, former cohabitant, fiancé, former fiancé, a person with whom the person making the calls has a child, or a person with whom the person making the calls has or had a dating relationship.

• *Other crimes and prohibitions.* A wide spectrum of statutes and ordinances may assist employers and law enforcement official in dealing with potential violence.

Law enforcement officials may be willing to prosecute threatening individuals for the mere act of having made the threats. California law, for example, prohibits threatening another with imminent violence, even if there is no intent of actually carrying out the threat. In fact, the threat is unlawful even if communicated to a third person who then communicates it to the intended victim. Individuals may also be charged and prosecuted for brandishing a weapon. California Penal Code Section 417 prohibits brandishing any type of deadly weapon in the presence of any other person in a "rude, angry, or threatening manner" or using such a weapon in a fight, except in self-defense.

Some states provide for increased criminal penalties if the perpetrator commits or attempts to commit a felony because of the victim's protected status. California law, for example, provides additional criminal penalties where the defendant commits or attempts to commit a felony because of the victim's race, color, religion, nationality, country of origin, ancestry, disability, or sexual orientation.

Special Liability Claims Involving Third Parties

Special Liability to Nonemployees for Conduct of Workers and Third Parties

In some states an employer is shielded from most employee claims growing out of injury or death on the job because the workers' compensation system provides the exclusive remedy for occupational injuries. Companies may, however, incur substantial liability to the survivors of employees, or even to nonemployees, for actions by individuals whose violent conduct could have been prevented.

On July 15, 1994, a California court of appeals upheld a jury award in excess of $5 millon against Cave Imaging Systems for negligently failing to protect a manager of a company for which Cave Imaging provided security services.[11] The manager was

[11] *Rosh v. Cave Imaging Systems, Inc.*, 26 Cal. App. 4th 1225 (1994) (petition for review denied).

shot and severely injured by a disgruntled employee who had been fired shortly before the shooting.

In January 1994, the owners of both a frozen yogurt shop and a mall in Austin, Texas, agreed to pay $12 million to the parents of four young girls. Two of the four victims worked in the store where they were murdered during a 1991 robbery. Although the crime was not solved, the civil suit successfully alleged inadequate security by the defendants.

In 1992, a Sonoma County, California, jury awarded $5.5 million in damages against a temporary agency to the survivors of a twenty-year-old woman stabbed to death on August 3, 1990, by a co-worker at the entrance of the winery where they both worked. The suspect, who had a criminal record, had been fired because of poor work habits. The temporary agency that assigned him to the winery had allegedly failed to check his work references.

Available remedies in such cases may include damages for emotional distress produced by the negligently caused injuries to the victims. In California, for example, emotional distress damages may be awarded to a plaintiff if the plaintiff is closely related to the injured victim, is present at the scene or the injury-producing event at the time it occurs and is then aware that is causing injury to the victim, and, as a result, suffer serious emotional distress.

Liability for Negligence Based on Foreseeable Criminal Activity

Courts are wrestling with whether workplace premises owners can be liable for negligence because of criminal activity by a visitor against an employee who works on the premises. Both the California Supreme Court and the District of Columbia Court of Appeals have attempted to define the premise owner's responsibility to protect workers. These courts have emphasized that the foreseeability of the criminal activity is a key factor in determining the owner's duty to safeguard the employees of companies located on the premises.

To establish negligence liability, the plaintiff must establish that the defendant owed the plaintiff a legal duty (i.e., protection), that the defendant breached the duty, and that the breach was a proximate or legal cause of plaintiff's injury. Courts have long recognized a landlord's duty to take reasonable steps to secure common areas against foreseeable criminal acts of third parties that are likely to occur in the absence of precautionary measures. The California Supreme Court held that the landlord's duty to protect tenants extends to the tenants' employees. In determining whether there is a duty, the California courts consider:

[The] foreseeability of harm to the plaintiff, the degree of certainty that the plaintiff suffered injury, the closeness of the connection between the defendant's conduct and the injury suffered, the moral blame attached to the defendant's conduct, the policy of preventing future harm, the extent of the burden to the defendant and consequences to the community of imposing a duty to exercise care with resulting liability for breach, and the availability, cost, and prevalence of insurance for the risk involved.

In the District of Columbia case, the court concluded that the employer was not liable for negligence even though some criminal activity had been reported in the vicinity of the store. As the manager was leaving the drugstore and walking toward the car where his wife was waiting, a Jaguar that had been parked farther away in the parking lot sped toward him and stopped. A man with a gun stepped out and demanded that the manager drop the bag he was carrying. The manager complied, but the robber fatally shot him. Thereafter, the wife sued the employer for failing to maintain a reasonably safe and secure environment and failing to provide adequate security.

The court stated that because the injury was directly caused by an intervening criminal act committed by an unknown third party, the employer would be liable only if the criminal act was so foreseeable that a duty arose to guard against it. The wife's failure to show that the murder was reasonably foreseeable meant in this case that the drugstore was not responsible for any negligence.

The magnitude, seriousness, and increasing frequency of

workplace violence compels employers to confront its reality. The problem cannot be ignored. Employers need to prepare to prevent and address this calamity. Knowledge of an employer's legal obligations is an essential first step. The next requires the preparation and implementation of appropriate policies and procedures for an effective response plan, which every employer should develop.

Chapter 6

Corporate Policies That Prevent Violence

Good policy manuals spell out the rules of the company. They define how people are expected to behave with co-workers and with customers, which is key to violence prevention. Good policies also define the procedures for responding to problematic situations that can escalate into violence, allowing all employees to be trained and prepared for resolving conflicts before violence occurs. A key part of any company violence prevention program is the development of policies and procedures that can keep situations from escalating into violence and that break down the denial of employees who see signs that an individual's behavior may lead to violence but fail to take them seriously.

Policies as Rules of Behavior That Prevent Violence

The murders you read about in the newspapers are only the tip of the iceberg of workplace violence. A study by the Northwestern National Life Insurance Company titled "Fear and Violence in the Workplace" found a great deal of workplace violence that fell short of homicide but that still had terrifying effects. Three percent of surveyed workers reported being physically attacked on the job. One in six workplace attacks involved a lethal weapon. Twenty-one percent of surveyed workers said that they knew a co-worker who had been threatened with physical harm during the past year. Dealing with customers is even more dangerous; twice as many physical attacks come from customers as from co-workers. The report concludes that nonlethal forms of violence, including harassment and intimidation, can be directly linked to worker burnout, lower productivity, and increased health care costs. They affect the health and productivity not only of the victims but also of the co-workers, who feel angry, fearful, stressed, and depressed as a result. According to the study, companies with effective policies on grievances, harassment, and other environmental safety issues report lower rates of workplace violence and lower levels of employee job dissatisfaction.

The report recommends ten ways a company's policies can be used to prevent or reduce workplace violence:

1. Foster a harmonious work environment.
2. Train supervisors and employees on how to resolve conflicts.
3. Develop effective polices to protect employees from harassment.
4. Establish procedures for handling grievances.
5. Provide job counseling for employees who are laid off or fired.
6. Train supervisors to recognize signs of a trouble employee.
7. Provide personal counseling through employee assistance programs.
8. Provide employee safety education programs.
9. Set up a crisis plan to deal with violent incidents.
10. Implement effective security procedures.

Companies that do a good job of preventing violence tend to have strong policies against harassment, effective grievance procedures, good security programs, a supportive work environment that gives employees adequate control over their work, open and trusting communication, and training in resolving conflicts through team building and negotiating skills. They have specific policies that clearly outline the rules of behavior that provide the foundation for the corporate environment. These are used to help shape the evolution of the company's culture in the desired direction. While policies should be written in consultation with lawyers, managers, line supervisors, and mental health, medical, employee assistance program (EAP), security, and human resource staff, they should be not so much documents designed to limit the company's liability as much as working documents that focus employee and management efforts on the environmental issues that can prevent workplace violence and create business success.

An important step in preventing workplace violence is the promulgation of policies designed to defuse volatile situations before they reach the point of violence. As you have read, many different sources of workplace conflict and distress have the potential to erupt into violence. Nearly all of these can be contained with proactive policies designed to prevent and used to intervene early in the spiral of behavior that can otherwise escalate into violence.

Policies Against Harassment and Intimidation

Company policies should state clearly that any form or manner of threatening remark or gesture in the workplace is unacceptable and that anyone who engages in such behavior will face disciplinary action, including possible removal from his job. There should be no tolerance for any threats of violence or intimidation by anyone at any level within a company. Just as airline personnel do not tolerate any implied references to bombs, a company should consider any actual or implied threat of violence as a real and serious danger. All threats should be thoroughly investigated.

The policy should require all employees, especially supervisors, to report to a specific manager every behavior of co-workers, customers, or anyone else at the worksite that could be taken as threatening or intimidating or that might lead to violence. Such reporting can occur only when expectations of the supervisor are clear, because co-workers, including supervisors and managers, frequently feel intimidated by direct or implicit threats. In addition, managers tend to deny the possibility of actual violence. It is amazing how often employees minimize the danger in these situations, in spite of the many warning signs that make the danger apparent. Corporate policy on reporting threats should make it clear that those employees who with good intentions provide such information will be protected from retaliation in any form. One way to protect them is to ensure that the reports are kept confidential. Another way is to ensure that the company neither fails to react nor overreacts to employee statements until it has gathered the facts about what really happened.

Often, there must be intervention before such situations can escalate into workplace violence. Early intervention in response to such threats is best, but it must be appropriate and based on the facts and on preplanned procedures. The more the company has prepared for the different scenarios it is likely to face, the faster and better able to respond it will be. For example, policies should define how the company will deal with an employee who will not discuss inappropriate behavior or cooperate in interventions designed to correct it.

Grievance Procedures

Many of the employees who have committed murder at the worksite were in the process of being disciplined or terminated by their employers. Disciplining and termination are two of the critical transition periods at work that present a high level of risk for potential violence. As a result, they also present a real opportunity to use appropriate violence prevention measures.

The single most important action a company can take to prevent violence around grievances is to ask itself, over and over, whether the disciplinary action is a punishment or an attempt to correct action and change behavior. This is a fundamental and basic question. The answer makes all the difference in the world. Punishment is punitive, provocative, and evocative of childlike behavior. Taking corrective action offers the possibility of the company's actions being supportive, reality-based, and positive. It allows a disciplinary action to become a learning opportunity and creates an atmosphere of trust, which is necessary for learning. Honest exchange and sharing develop mutual understanding, rather than adversarial showdowns and standoffs. Both parties win, rather than having a winner and a loser. Unless both sides in the work environment feel successful, there is a failure or loss for both the company and the employee. Creating "win-win" solutions is possible in many more situations than people imagine.

Clear written policies regarding possible violence must be developed, especially for the human resources staff and for managers involved in terminating workers and handling formal grievances. Disciplinary action raises the level of stress in most employees; such events spiral into different ways of thinking, feeling, and, sometimes, acting. Supporting the employee's belief that she has the resources to cope with the situation and thus relieving the stress is critical to de-escalating the potential for violence. In order to do this, you must approach the disciplinary action in a way that seeks to understand the employee's point of view: "Why do you think this is being done? How do you understand the problem? Why do you think your boss sees this as a problem? What do you see as options and solutions?" These questions are designed to communicate a desire to understand, to empathize, and to help the employee cope with the situation. They are neither punitive in tone nor intended to avoid the real issues. They are designed to help the employee see the supervisor's point of view and to come to mutually palatable solutions.

It is also important that employees, especially those who are being disciplined or terminated, have a constructive mechanism to vent their frustrations and anger. Managers need to be trained to use neutral and nonprovocative tones in informing employees of the reasons for their being disciplined or terminated. In addition, employers should consider giving employees the opportunity to submit grievances in response to any disciplinary, punitive, or potentially terminal action by the company. Creating a grievance procedure allows employees to vent their anger by completing a grievance form. By the time an angry employee finishes writing a grievance, her anger may well have dissipated. At the least, the employee will have had to create a rationale for her reaction and perceptions. This allows the employee to reflect on her own thinking and gives the manager or human resources professional the opportunity to better understand the employee's subjective experience and her thinking about the problem. For these reasons, companies should ask for written responses to grievances, but never as a substitute for discussing the situation with the individual in person.

Because being disciplined and facing the threat or reality of termination is always stress-evoking for an employee, the persons initiating and presenting the action should always consider referring the employee to an Employee Assistance Program or to an outside counseling resource shortly after or at the time of the action. Such confidential assistance can offer support to frustrated or troubled employees in dealing with their problems. It can help them connect with the psychological or substance abuse treatment they may need, and it can be a valuable outlet for those who might otherwise resort to violence to communicate real or perceived grievances.

My father always told me to expect the best and prepare for the worst. You should always do your homework before a formal grievance hearing or other highly tense meeting so that you know how the other person is coping and what reaction to expect. Still, there will be times when you don't have all the facts or when the situation has changed without your knowing it. Accordingly, when having grievance or other special meetings, always give some consideration to security precautions, such as checking the room arrangement, exits, and view access and considering the possibility that weapons may be present. You should also know the standard safety procedures, including knowing codes for alerting other staff or the police, ensuring that staff is knowledgeable about what to do in an emergency, and having a relationship and an agreement with security personnel and the local police department, should they need to be called. The room should be private and not too small.

Questions you should ask while preparing for potentially conflicted meetings include:

- Are there pieces of furniture or other items that could potentially be used as weapons?
- Are the ashtrays made of paper or cardboard, or are they glass?
- Are there framed pictures or posters on the walls?

- Are there pencils, pens, or hardcover books lying about?
- Is staff too secluded during this interview? (At a mini-mum, staff should be warned to leave doors open during any potentially dangerous interview.)

One last, important consideration in avoiding violence at disciplinary hearings is never to make discipline or termination a surprise. Clear communication along the way should have pre-pared the employee for the action. She should even expect it and have a realistic outlook on it. Companies that have good psychological and performance evaluations help prepare em-ployees to expect the actions that are taken, making them less punitive and more fact-based and making them seem less precip-itous to the employee. Such assessments can be extended to cur-rent employees through behavioral observations and supervi-sory inputs, as well.

Terminating Employees Safely

When separating an employee for cause or poor performance, a company should follow a systematic process of documentation. Regular performance appraisals are an excellent tool for alerting an employee and his supervisor to a potential problem. If the performance problem is not corrected, the appraisal can docu-ment that the employee was advised and given an opportunity to improve. Be sure to document written and oral feedback for at least six months before the termination to protect both parties.

The number of stupid ways that bosses find to fire their employees is incredible. Many incidents of workplace violence are perpetrated by recently terminated employees who feel wronged and humiliated and who return to seek revenge even months after leaving the job. One trucker went on a violent ram-page when he was fired after being told by his supervisor that "guys like you are a dime a dozen." That was the final straw.

I was on a national television show with a call-in from Michi-gan. The man owned four dry cleaning stores, and one of his managers had begun threatening to kill him. The threats seemed part of a series of events that indicated that the fellow was struggling to keep his head above water. On the show, another expert on workplace violence told the owner that it was a clear-cut situation. He had simply to fire the manager who was making the threats as soon as possible to get rid of him. The error and the potentially disastrous consequences of this poor advice are evident if you understand that increasing stress on an individual increases the possibility that he will become violent. If the manager was already having a crisis and summarily lost his job, it would be only a small step for him to decide that the owner was trying to hurt him and, in a rage, to act on his earlier threats. It would be much wiser for the owner to get this man the professional help that could stabilize and defuse his anger and confusion before resolving the employment situation. It is very naive to think that you can protect yourself from problematic employees by firing them; yet many managers think exactly that way. Employees who are on disability or who are terminated have come back months after leaving the company and taken revenge. Out of sight is not out of mind for them.

It behooves an employer never to surprise an individual with a termination action; it is wise always to give ample warning of such dramatic action. The steps leading up to the termination should prepare the individual for what is going to happen. Attempts should always be made before hand to understand what is going on inside the person and what her external situation is. Getting help and support to help her deal with the action should always be considered.

The employee who is being fired should always feel that she has recourse. It is when a person feels powerless and hopeless and believes that there is nothing else she can do that feelings of desperation or retaliation take over. The opportunity to talk or to stay in touch with an appropriate person in the company can stave off a sense of isolation and rejection. Providing medical benefits continued so that the employee can get help if needed may be money well spent. The idea that you can simply and quickly wash your hands of the whole mess is misleading.

The way in which you end someone's employment is very important in preventing violence and often in lowering wrongful termination suits. In Chapter 9, I outline the correct processes to accomplish this, whether you are terminating one person or hundreds. There is no question that these are highly charged situations. All you have to do is listen to the language used by those taking the actions to understand the raw and primitive emotions that are involved: "We shot him. We took him out." These issues are a matter of life and death for many people.

Establishing Clear Channels for Communicating Threats

Large and medium-size companies should have clear written policies regarding the chain of command for communicating direct and veiled threats of violence from workers. It is very easy for others to either minimize or be intimidated by threats, so communication channels must be confidential and clear. Supervisors should know who to tell in management and who on the medical or human resources staff should receive referrals for further evaluation. Effective communication means that someone sees it as his job to listen to employees in distress closely enough to assess whether he should follow up on the person through an appropriate referral. That is not gossip; it is open communication in an environment committed to enhancing safety and to responding to its employees constructively.

Many experts recommend a communication channel that bypasses supervisors. After a shooting at the Royal Oaks, Michigan, post office brought a change in company policy that emphasized the need to take threats seriously, 328 tips that merited investigation were received, and seven employees were arrested. Employees must know that their companies take threats seriously and will take confidential but appropriate and swift action when there is a real danger. Many employees threatened by a co-worker do not tell their supervisors for fear of retaliation by the co-worker. Human resources staff, employee assistance counselors, security personnel, or a confidential hotline can supplement or replace supervisors as resources for those receiving threats. The eventual goal is to eliminate threats. In the meantime, it is important to surface problems for preventive investigation and action.

Violence Response Team Assessment Policy

Every company should have a policy on procedures for assessing threats and the potential for workplace violence and for minimizing the possibility that a threatening situation will escalate into violence. The policy should outline sources and early warning signs of potential violence, appropriate responses to early warning signs and threats, follow-up steps, and general prevention strategies. Because threatening situations can come in many varieties, this plan should not be presented as a cookbook to be followed rigidly but rather as an informative guide. As risks arise and evolve, the plan should provide the basis for the specific actions necessary for resolving them and for reducing their impact on company employees and their families.

The company violence response team, which is described in detail in Chapter 7, helps carry out assessment plans by investigating all reports of threatening or violent behavior. Like reports of harassment and intimidation, all reports of such behavior should be thoroughly and promptly investigated and the investigation documented. In addition, if violence or threats are found to have occurred, immediate steps should be taken to eliminate any risk resulting from them and any possible recurrence. Indifference to threats of violence can often lead to significant corporate liability. For example, in 1982 a woman and several co-workers were shot in a San Francisco office building by the woman's husband, who had made threats for months before the attack. The woman had alerted her employer to the threats, but neither the company nor building management had taken any steps to protect the employees. The woman and the injured co-workers recovered about $7 million from the employer and building management after suing for negligence.

Consider, for example, an employee who, after an argument, has threatened to assault a co-worker. The situation is evaluated and reviewed by the response team to determine the level of risk involved and the next steps, if any, that are required to resolve the conflict. The employee is assessed and probably physically removed by transfer from the co-worker's presence, if possible. If an employee threatens to harm a co-worker but says that she has a treatable mental condition that causes erratic behavior, the employer has an obligation to investigate whether the condition caused the threats and can be controlled by medication or other treatment. Such an investigation includes contacting the employee's physician or having an independent fitness-for-duty evaluation. The ADA places a significant risk of liability on companies that attempt to terminate employees in a situation where their disability is not currently under control but could be controlled with proper treatment. Apart from the demands of the law, it is not safe for the company to attempt to terminate employees who are threatening harm and who are out of control instead of helping them to be restabilized. All of these contingencies and procedures should be laid out in the company's assessment policy.

The same principle holds for customer threats. When a conflict has been identified, a genuine attempt by a manager to contact the customer should be made to try to defuse the situation. However, if the customer persists in his threats, the person should be reported to the police and employees should be advised to call a supervisor or the police if the customer appears at the worksite. By treating these situations seriously and documenting all actions taken in response to them, the employer is not only able to defer many potentially violent conflicts but also creates proof that she acted reasonably to try to prevent any violence from occurring, a key issue should a lawsuit emerge from a later violent incident.

Employees should also be trained to respond to a violent attack just as they would for other emergencies like fires or medical crises. Emergency phone numbers, escape routes, self-defense maneuvers, and security procedures should be listed and readily available.

The company should also have guidelines on when, in the face of threats, it will recommend and pay for voluntary therapy for the individual, when it will seek involuntary hospital commitment, when it will warn potential victims, and when it will call the police. Policies should spell out how to use restraining orders and how to cope with domestic violence that spills into the workplace. Most of all, policies should create a perception of fair and just treatment across the board on every aspect of employee treatment and should encourage consistent, steady responses to risks of violence.

Physical Security

Since violence is so difficult to predict with accuracy, it becomes very important to do whatever can be done to prevent it. Providing adequate physical security is one method of prevention, and how a company is addressing this area should be laid out in its policies about security.

First, it is important to secure the premises from crime by outsiders. Employers should pay attention to the dangers of conventional violence, such as armed robberies, which account for the majority of workplace homicides. Employers have a responsibility to install safety features in areas where employees are especially vulnerable to attacks. Security guards and emergency police alarms can be put in place where employees work alone and security fences and lighting installed in dark parking lots. Second, companies should secure their facilities from activities that increase risk for employees. For instance, companies should insist on the right to search lockers and cars, and these rights should be well publicized in an effort to prevent problems that could lead to violence.

While it is important to evaluate physical security, there is a danger in overemphasizing this method of prevention. I once spoke with a manager at a well-known package goods company. She described how the executives on the third floor of the corporate headquarters had recently installed electronic locking systems on all office doors in case a disgruntled employee or customer were to come after them with a gun. The not-so-funny joke going on the second floor, where all the midlevel managers were located, was: "I guess they don't care if we get shot. Maybe we should put up signs on our floor pointing potential gunmen to the stairs that lead to the third floor!" A concern for security can provoke a bunker mentality and become demoralizing and even dangerous. In this company, it fit with the perception by many managers that senior management was indifferent to their needs and feelings, which created considerable resentment.

Education and Training

The best time for dealing with threats and risk is before the need arises. Policies should lay out due process so that they are perceived as consistent, equitable, and honest. An employee handbook should describe clearly and simply what employee conduct is expected and what is not allowed. Wide distribution of the handbook among employees will help develop the perception of fairness among workers. The handbook should explicitly state that threats of violence and bodily harm and intimidation by employees will not be tolerated and constitute grounds for termination. It should also say that the company reserves the right in such situations to have an evaluation by a professional to determine fitness for duty.

Company policies should also make clear who an employee should notify if she receives or sees such a threat, how to get assistance in dealing with the effect it has on her, and the duty of each employee to warn and to protect potential victims. Courses of action should be spelled out and can include fitness-for-duty exams, disability leaves, leaves of absence, reassignments, performance counseling, terminations, and restraining orders. These policies have the dual benefit of helping prevent violence and reducing corporate liability. Staff should be educated about how to use these guidelines, and compliance should be audited.

The company must support its supervisors and managers in effectively confronting inappropriate behavior. Because high-risk employees are often successful in intimating their bosses and co-workers, clear policies and personal support are needed to short-circuit behavior before it can escalate. Remember, the sooner potentially violent behavior is dealt with, the less likely it is to escalate. Early identification and intervention are key to preventing violence. Using appropriate resources requires confrontation, which is a big hurdle for many managers. Supervisors instead tend to insulate the employee, allowing the behavior to continue and, perhaps, to escalate. Avoiding the problem this way sends the message that the behavior is condoned by the company. Instead, performance reviews should always address such behaviors. Reviews can be an effective front-line defense against potential escalation. Supervisory training should cover how to perform effective performance reviews, how to confront dysfunctional behavior without escalating it, and how to recognize and respond to at-risk employees, including how to refer employees to suitable counselors. Supervisors should also have the opportunity to receive education on conflict resolution, mediation, and effective communication techniques. Every level of management plays an important role in identifying and handling potential or actual violence within a company and should be trained to do so.

Some companies have "toxic" supervisors who can't confront effectively. These are supervisors who have been seduced into feeling powerful at the expense of others because of their own experiences with authoritarian figures. In an uncertain job market, their subordinates are likely to take even subtle threats to their jobs very seriously and perhaps even as life-or-death situations. It is easy for them to feel unfairly treated or pushed into a corner by a domineering supervisor who flaunts his power and control over them.

The role of the human resources staff includes developing clear guidelines for terminating workers and handling formal grievances, keeping in mind the possibility of violence. Maintaining good employee records, developing appropriate security precautions, having employee assistance services and procedures for bringing in expert consultants in high-risk situations, and training supervisors to be effective all depend on having clear policies and procedures for handling potentially volatile or threatening situations.

A company's policies should define a specialized role for its violence response team to provide education and training to employees in how to prevent violence. Education should take the form of providing some general knowledge of mental disorders and substance abuse and special knowledge of risk assessment in particular. Because there is no national legal standard for assessing risk, companies must know the local legal standards and communicate the relevant laws of their jurisdiction regarding steps to follow when a positive assessment is made.

It is important to have a team of staff or consultants familiar with risk assessment, including predictor and criterion variables, true and false positives and negatives, decision rules, base rates, and key findings of current risk assessment research. The company should also have one person responsible as "risk educator" to help keep the company current and focused on these issues. This person should see that there is a postincident analysis of situations involving threatened or actual violence. The company can use this analysis to determine the effectiveness of the interventions it is using and to improve its policies, procedures, training efforts, and company responses.

An assessment policy should define how the violence response team should go about gathering relevant information in assessing risk in a given situation. Enough accurate data must be gathered to develop a plan for action. Sources of data can include

- Interviews with the employee to discover any history, plans, or thoughts about violence
- Interviewing significant others to see if they are concerned that the employee might hurt someone
- Interviews with supervisors and other employees
- Reviews of the employee's current and past records, especially of violence or threats of violence.

The violence response team must resolve the conflict between the individual's right to confidentiality and preservation of reputation and respect, on one hand, and the safety of others, on the other. All employees deserve and need due process. But the company also has an obligation to the manager or co-worker who could be the target of threats. While assessing situations for risk, the violence response team can also be effective in helping make the company environment less prone to violence. Through

its questioning, it can reshape provocative and unacceptable behavior. A tendency to blow off steam can be redirected by a
requirement for a fitness-for-duty assessment. Training for employees should include how to identify the warning signs as well
as, equally important, how to react appropriately and without
violating the employee's rights or escalating the situation.

Chapter 7

Responding to Actual Risk Situations: The Company Violence Response Team

An essential ingredient in preventing violence on the job is identifying and responding to high-risk situations before they become violent. I have heard many horror stories from businesspeople in both large and small companies about potentially threatening employee situations they have faced. A group of human resources managers from a small bank association described a typical array of conflicts. One woman manager told the story of an employee who was going through a very difficult divorce. Her estranged husband was beginning to show up at the bank after work. The manager didn't know how to help the woman because her counselor was telling her not to seek a restraining order for fear it could provoke the husband to violence. The husband was appearing with more frequency and in an increasingly ominous way that was frightening other employees.

A second banker described an employee who had suddenly become withdrawn and very tense. It was known that the person was having some severe personal financial problems, but he had never seemed unstable before. A third banking professional described the increasing fear her employees were feeling as the area around the bank was deteriorated and experienced a significant increase in crime, including a holdup at a store nearby.

How Do I Know If I Have a Real Risk Situation?

It is impossible to know which of these situations represent a genuine risk of becoming violent, because, as in most situations, little information is available initially and because violence is difficult to predict. I therefore encourage companies to err on the side of providing support and of giving attention to every threatening situation. Only after you have quietly gathered additional facts about the situation can you decide if it is necessary to intervene and, if so, select the most appropriate method of doing so. In order to do this fact-finding, every company needs to have a violence response team in place. No individual can serve this function alone because of the complexity, the emotional intensity, and the potential liability involved. For large corporations, the team is primarily internal. For small companies, it may be composed mostly of outside resources.

What Is a Risk Situation?

The violence response team should have a clearly stated policy of responding to every threat of violence and every dangerous situation that surfaces. This should be done via a process that corresponds to the cyclical way that behavior escalates into violence. The response team should:

1. Conduct an initial risk assessment of the individual and the situation.

2. Develop an initial action plan that includes notifying potential resources, reviewing available information, and determining investigative and further fact-gathering steps.

3. Defuse the individual's stress.

4. Review available facts and refine action plans; consult with experts on the team; review security requirements; reevaluate as facts come forward; and plan further actions on the basis of these new facts. Interventions may include the use of restraining orders and other protective, controlling measures for the employee, for co-workers, and for potential victims.

5. Set time frames for follow-up and referral for problem solving and reassessment.

By assessing the issues quickly and at the beginning of the difficulty, the response team can deal with a developing problem before it becomes a crisis. It can work closely with the employee's and the supervisor's behavior before either escalates into violence. It can use a variety of types of evaluations, such as fitness-for-duty assessments, to gather additional information on the level of risk a person presents and to get help for the person. In extreme situations, it can use involuntary hospitalization and police injunctions.

The team also needs to identify and help protect potential victims. It can help the manager or supervisor deal with his own frustration, anger, anxiety, and fear so that he can maintain the perspective and balance to deal with the employee in appropriate ways.

How a Violence Response Team Works

To illustrate how a violence response team can work within your company, let me walk you through the step-by-step process of a real-life example. Remember, the overall role of the response team is to assess potentially violent situations in the workplace and to develop a course of action to de-escalate and resolve the situations while protecting potential victims.

Here is a sample scenario:

1. A manager in a financial services company is approached by an employee, who says that the man sitting at the desk next to hers has begun to act in a very strange manner. He is overheard talking to himself, mumbling quietly about people being out to hurt him. He is also acting more withdrawn and anxious. Today he has said something to a small group of employees in his department that implies he might hurt them. It is known that he had a performance review two weeks earlier that was quite tense, and it is suspected that the company may be considering firing him.

2. The manager has been trained to call the coordinator of the violence response team. In some companies this role is filled by an employee assistance person; in other companies a medical or human resources person handles these duties. The manager gives the coordinator the facts as she has them, repeating what the co-worker has said as much verbatim as possible and filling in some further facts about recent deterioration in the employee's job performance.

3. The violence response team coordinator immediately begins an investigation. He privately interviews the person who reported the incident as well as the other two employees who heard the threat. These interviews are held away from the work area and are done quietly and confidentially. Those interviewed are asked to keep the discussion to themselves. He gathers as much information as possible about what was actually said and done and about the employee in question. All information that is available at this point is documented in detail and as factually as possible, apart from impressions and interpretations by others.

4. The response team coordinator reviews the information to decide if further action is necessary. He reviews it with the human resources director (in some companies, it could be with the medical director or an outside expert) and documents his decision and plan. The plan often identifies what specific additional data are needed to assess the risk and what immediate supports could be provided to the employee.

5. If the facts include any of the warning signs for violence or there is a reasonable cause to believe that the situation could escalate further, the coordinator activates the response team to gather additional data if necessary, to plan a course of action, and to monitor the plan's progress in controlling the situation.

6. In conjunction with medical staff or an outside adviser, the team develops plans to investigate and intervene. One course of action may include gathering more information about the employee, in particular information on how the employee responds to stress, how he sees his current work and life situation, how he is feeling about it, and what actions he might be considering taking. Warning signs of violence will also be investigated.

7. The appropriate team member is selected to interview the person who reported the threat and any others who can verify or provide additional information on the employee's state of mind. This is done discreetly so as not to alert the potentially violent employee. The person then also interviews the employee, if warranted. Security is arranged for this interview if it is believed the employee could become enraged or is about to become violent. Security personnel in this company are experienced and trained to handle these situations in a calm, low-key manner that de-escalates and supports the individual, rather than threatening him. If it were otherwise, security's behavior could precipitate violence.

In this case, it is clear that the employee is experiencing significant distress. During the interview, he seems relieved to have the opportunity to talk about his dilemma with an empathetic ear. After hearing that the conversation is designed to respond to his distress, he is very forthcoming about how terribly upset he is. He is afraid he is going to lose his job, has been hearing vague noises in his head, and can't concentrate on his work. His wife has recently left him for another man. He tells the interviewer that he doesn't know which way to turn or what to do. He feels he may be losing control. He has thoughts about killing himself or his wife and is feeling irritated by people around him, especially women. He does not have a gun but is thinking of getting one.

8. These interviews are documented in a separate file and reviewed by the response team to determine if the individual is a threat to himself or to others. Since he is not in imminent danger of hurting anyone, a decision is made to refer him for counseling. A meeting with an employee assistance counselor is scheduled for that evening. (If the response team or an outside expert consultant had decided that the individual was an immediate danger to himself or others, the team would have made different decisions, perhaps involving law enforcement agencies, obtaining a temporary restraining order, implementing security plans, or even seeking involuntary psychiatric hospitalization.) The team also makes a determination about the employee's continued work status. For some employees, a leave of absence may help

by removing them from an environment they find stressful. For others, being put off the job, even temporarily, may confirm their worst fears and push them to take desperate measures.

9. It is also the responsibility of the response team to provide appropriate information and support to the victims and/or targets of an employee's threats. In this situation, it is determined that the man's co-workers are more concerned than alarmed by what they have been seeing. (If there had been an immediate threat to one of them, the company would have had to make clear efforts to protect that person from harm.)

10. As time goes on, the violence response team continues to be involved in gathering data, planning interventions, and reassessing the effect of those interventions until there is a final disposition of the risk of violence. Actions can include helping those affected by the employee's threats as well as the employee himself.

About one week after the initial incident, the man shares with several of his work group that he has started to get help from a counselor for some personal problems. He tells them he is sorry about the way he treated them. He also tells his manager that he is temporarily taking some medication that is helping him to concentrate better and to stay calmer at work. The team continues to monitor his condition for another four weeks, until it is sure he is stable and out of danger. The employee assistance counselor he is seeing obtains permission from the employee to communicate his general status to the response team coordinator during this time.

Does all of this effort work? An assessment team at IBM is convened whenever a threat is made. It evaluates the problem and takes appropriate action, including using law enforcement agencies. Since initiating this effort, IBM reports a significant reduction in the severity of threatening incidents.

Best Practices: A Corporate Model

A large company headquartered on the East Coast has established a process for investigating and resolving all incidents in which it believes a threat to persons or property has occurred. To this end, it has developed expert violence response teams at its corporate headquarters, at each of its divisional headquarters, and in every geographical region.

Each team includes experts in security, occupational health, law, employee assistance, employee relations, and forensics. The process the team uses to investigate and manage an alleged threat is fluid and depends on the specific situation. Generally, it uses the following strategies:

1. It conducts an initial risk assessment to:
   - Determine the level of response required
   - Lay out the steps it will follow to investigate the situation
2. It develops an initial action plan that includes:
   - Notification of resource teams to become involved in intervening
   - Review of available information
   - Determination of further investigative and fact-gathering steps
3. It reviews the available facts and refines its action plan, including:
   - Evaluating and implementing a plan to protect the commercial interests of the company, to support any potential victims, and to remove any threat to the office
4. It assigns members of the team to:
   - Consult with an expert to provide guard or twenty-four-hour protection service, to obtain a temporary restraining order, to gain appropriate family involvement, and to notify those who need to know
   - Review security requirements and safety precautions
   - Determine notification requirements
   - Establish privacy protection and communications procedures
   - Determine and involve employee assistance program support requirements
   - Determine and engage occupational/medical health support requirements
5. It re-evaluates as facts come forward and plans new inter-

ventions and actions to be taken on the basis of the evolving facts.

6. The company has debriefing teams that after every episode is resolved:
   - Review the facts and the actions taken
   - Determine what can be learned from how the situation was handled
   - Support the team members who participated

How to Set Up a Violence Response Team in Your Company

Whether yours is a large corporation or a small business, you need to have a violence response team available. The team should plan preventive measures, train your employees in how to implement them, and be prepared to intervene at the very earliest phase of a potentially explosive situation in order to de-escalate it. Depending on your company's particular situation, your team may be staffed by employees, external consultants, or some combination of the two. The size of your business is one consideration in making the decision on how to staff. If you have a small business, you probably already have working relationships with professionals with whom you consult, such as your lawyer and security firm. They have the potential to be part of your violence response team. If you work in a large corporation, you probably have internal professionals in these areas of responsibility. In either situation, you cannot automatically assume that the professionals you work with have the special expertise you need to perform this function. These are the people who will put together your policies and procedures to prevent violence and review responses to situations as they arise. The team should include relevant specialists and all vested stockholders. This ensures that all critical perspectives and functional areas of responsibility or liability are involved in each case so that you have your bases covered.

There are several areas of expertise that must be represented on a well-functioning violence response team and several questions you will want to ask to determine if you can use the resources you already have or need to develop new ones. Typical positions to be filled on such a team include:

• *Violence response team coordinator.* Has overall responsibility for assessing individuals and their potential victims. Sometimes this includes doing or obtaining background checks on the individual; providing crisis intervention or at least appropriate support to the individual or to co-workers; and developing, documenting, and implementing a suitable action plan.

The kind of skills this person needs include a calm and steady personality, good judgment about people, an ability to ask for help rather than go it alone, and an interest and training in crisis assessment and management. Because this person needs to be seen as an employee advocate, or at least as a neutral and fair party, a human resources person is often selected, if she has the other requisite skills as well.

• *Employee assistance program counselor.* Oversees and coordinates the delivery of professional assistance to the person at risk. These supports can include crisis intervention, threat assessment, clinical counseling, and treatment of chemical dependency. In some situations, the counselor provides the service firsthand; in other cases, she refers the person to local clinical professionals who provide treatment.

The EAP counselor needs to have solid training in risk assessment and crisis intervention. Many psychotherapists do not have this expertise, so be cautious about credentials and experience in selecting a professional for this role. He also needs to understand the laws on confidentiality, involuntary commitment, and protection of potential victims in the jurisdiction in which your company is located. In many larger companies with formal employee assistance programs, the violence response team coordinator and the counselor are the same person.

• *Plant, line, or operational manager.* Ensures identification of the threat initially and monitors the individual's response to implementation of the action plan. He provides the resources needed to handle the situation and assumes responsibility for the overall outcome of the interventions. Because workplace violence is really a business issue and many of its preventive aspects are related directly to the success of the business, it is important to have line management involved in a key role.

The types of skills this person needs to have include an understanding of the impact of how people are treated on their behavior, good and unbiased judgment about people, and the ability to set limits and enforce fair rules while at the same time being empathic and kind. This is the kind of person who is easy to talk to, who is not easily flustered, who can calm an escalating temper, but who also takes action in a direct fashion. The better this person's working relationships with employees before an incident, the more effective he will be.

• *Medical personnel/occupational nurse.* Assists in the assessment of the potentially violent situation, including reviewing appropriate medical records and coordinating the medical and injury compensation information that may be required. She assesses and makes recommendations about the potential risk of violence and appropriate courses of potential action, including fitness-for-duty exams, leaves of absence, and hospitalizations.

This individual needs to have a good working knowledge of the medical practices and legal issues involved in various job actions that can be taken. She needs to be comfortable dealing with individuals who are in a higher-than-usual state of agitation and persuasive in exploring options that the employee can find acceptable.

• *Legal counsel/labor relations specialist.* Provides input on how to deal with the employee's present work status; reviews the background of the employee's work-related conflicts; considers factors such as pending disciplinary, ADA, or equal employment opportunity complaints; and provides input on contractual or legal procedures relating to the course of action to be taken, such as termination.

This person must have expertise in the employment laws of the particular area where your company or division is located. She also needs to know the laws related to corporate and personal liability as they relate to workplace violence, confidentiality, involuntary hospitalization, and case law on actions that must be taken to protect potential victims.

• *Security service firm representative.* Assists in the selection process by obtaining background checks and criminal records of applicants, assesses physical security issues for the company, and performs investigations and other appropriate functions as incidences surface.

It is important that the rep not have a "Dick Tracy" attitude toward employees. He should be part of a company that carefully screens and trains new recruits and that takes a proactive stance toward security, actively and visibly developing relationships with employees in a cordial manner that characterizes the security service workers as safety agents, rather than enforcers or cops. It is also important that they be familiar with local police and emergency services and be able to negotiate response agreements with law enforcement officers before they are needed.

• *Forensic consultant/adviser.* Assesses the potential of threat situations and recommends a course of action to the violence response team. She provides second opinions and outside expertise. Because high-risk situations generally create a significant level of emotional intensity and provide only limited data on which to make decisions, a company lowers its liability and develops better action plans to resolve risk situations by having a forensic mental health specialist available to review individual situations and to make specific recommendations.

These psychologists or psychiatrists should have special training and experience in high-risk situations in business settings. They should be readily available, both at the site and by phone. They should be effective at facilitation, problem solving, and lowering anxiety.

The members of the violence response team must all be good at interacting with one another while under pressure and at creative problem solving. They must have the skills to provide training for managers, supervisors, and employees periodically as part of the company's preventive efforts. They must be able to develop and revise the company's policies regarding violence prevention and response. They must have the calm and good judgment that allows them to review high-risk situations and to evaluate the interventions that were used as part of a continual improvement effort.

Assessing the Individual for Risk of Violence

Early Intervention and the Role of the Supervisor

Experts agree that there are two key elements that can prevent a potentially violent employee from escalating to the level of action: (1) recognizing the early warning signs and (2) quickly intervening to assist the employee and protect potential victims. Any delay in addressing an incident or early warning indicators may confuse an increasingly unstable employee and send a message that her erratic behavior is acceptable. The delay may also allow the individual to take further advantage of the situation and allow her to spin out of control instead of receiving the help she needs.

Given this reality, it is apparent that the first-line supervisor or manager plays a crucial role in observing changes in an employee and in identifying and responding to the early warning signs of potential violence. While there is no foolproof system for predicting who will become violent, it is essential that your front-line supervisors and managers be trained and held accountable for knowing the early warning signs, recognizing them when they occur, notifying the appropriate resources, and responding in appropriate ways.

Warning Signs of Potential Workplace Violence

You are endangering yourself and your employees if you use a particular stereotype of the violence-prone person to predict which employee may become violent. Warning signs can be misused in the same way. They can lull you into a false sense of security. Sometimes a person whose behavior does not match your list of warning signs may nonetheless become violent.

The violent individual almost always exhibits warning signs before actually becoming violent. Please remember, however, that it is not possible to predict with certainty any individual's risk for violence. Warning signs should be used only to provoke you into assessing a particular individual and situation, using your growing knowledge about how violence occurs.

Also keep in mind that violence always occurs in a context that the violent individual perceives to be nonresponsive and threatening. It escalates over time in the spiral of stress and mental and emotional reactions that lead to violent actions. Certain occasions (e.g., the grievance and termination processes discussed in Chapter 6, some types of organizational environments as described in Chapter 8, and major changes such as the downsizing discussed in Chapter 9) are always stressful for the employees involved and are therefore capable of provoking violence. These are the contexts in which it is especially important to listen more carefully and more often than usual to employees, especially if you see any of the following behavior:

1. Threatening statements to kill or do harm to self or to others
   - Verbal threats
     - Stated intention to hurt or kill someone
     - Repeated threatening statements/constant swearing at others
     - Statements like "I understand why the guy did what he did at the post office"
     - Talk about harming self or others, with detailed threats
   - Pattern of escalating threats that appear well planned
   - References to other incidents of workplace violence
   - A preoccupation with violence and expressed ideas about acting in a similar fashion

2. Intimidating behavior
   - Intimidating co-workers or supervisors; reports from co-workers about their fear of the employee
   - Exhibiting insubordination or open defiance; challenging of authority
   - Crossing behavioral boundaries in an inappropriate and repeated fashion with another person, including excessive phone calls, messages, letters or memos, office appearances, following or stalking, or gift-giving
   - Being confrontational; appearing angry, easily provoked, impulsive, unpredictable, restless, agitated

- Acting belligerently toward customers
- Blaming others for everything that goes wrong, never having a sense of one's own responsibility

3. History of violent, reckless, or antisocial behavior
   - Evidence of prior assaultive behavior (e.g., spousal abuse or military misconduct)

4. Alleged fondness for firearms
   - Fascination with weapons, service in military or law enforcement
   - Easy access to firearms and ammunition

5. Recent marked performance decline
   - Attendance problems or absences from work assignment
   - Decreased productivity and inconsistent work patterns
   - Concentration problems
   - Increased involvement in accidents
   - Continual excuses, inability to accept responsibility for even the most inconsequential errors

6. Changes in personality
   - Withdrawal
   - Change from introversion to boisterous behavior
   - Sudden and dramatic changes in behavior (e.g., increasing anger and agitation)
   - Major changes in interpersonal relations
   - Decline in personal grooming

7. Major changes in mood or behavior
   - Experiencing bizarre thoughts or paranoid behavior, including psychotic thoughts
   - Having fantasies with self-centered outcomes
   - Having irrational violent associations or thoughts
   - Making delusional commands or statements (e.g., referencing UFOs, predicting the end of the world, being spied upon, seeing strange things)
   - Displaying secretive behavior
   - Writing poems or letters that are bizarre or make reference to violence

- Feeling that one is being singled out or fear that a person is out to get one
- Experiencing strong emotional mood swings
- Receiving unconventional religious messages
- Making a change in level of contact, such as going into someone's office too often, filing too many grievances, following an individual home or to the parking lot
- Experiencing severe depression

8. Obsessions
   - Desire to hurt a specific person or group
   - A romantic attachment to someone, not necessarily a sexual attachment
   - Preoccupation with a notoriously violent incident
   - Obsession with weapons, including owning a gun or gun collection, fascination with weapons, subscriptions to gun magazines like *Soldier of Fortune*, proficiency in gun use

9. Serious stress in the employee's personal life
   - Financial problems
   - Crying, excessive personal phone calls
   - Losses (job, marriage, loved one)
   - Personal problems (e.g., divorce, bankruptcy, anything leading to high level of stress)
   - Desperation

10. Substance abuse (drugs or alcohol) leading to:
    - Impaired reasoning ability
    - Social inhibition
    - Diminished ability to distinguish right from wrong
    - Sudden lying or concealing of information
    - Agitation and paranoia

How to Do Threat Assessment

The role of the front-line supervisor, the manager, and the violence response team coordinator is not to do the kind of detailed threat assessment that a forensic expert would do but to gather sufficient data to determine if the employee represents enough of a real risk to initiate the use of the team and its resources. To begin their assessment, the supervisor, manager, and violence team coordinator can:

1. Investigate the interactional factors between the employee and others involved in the situation, such as:
   - Both sides' body language and tone of voice
   - Employee's present ability to carry out the threat
   - Employee's propensity to engage in physical violence
   - The event that caused the employee to react
   - The context in which words were used by the employee
   - The response and reaction of the potential target
   - The employee's subsequent conduct (e.g., remorse, concern, desire to correct or rectify the situation)
2. Collect data from the individual's personnel and medical records and from other employees, supervisors, and outside sources as appropriate in order to identify any prior incidents as well as any current turbulence in the person's life.
3. If appropriate, obtain professional clinical input on psychological factors affecting the employee.
4. Using outside resources if necessary, begin to defuse the situation and to determine what further actions are required. A need for clinical intervention may be identified, particularly in the case of a threatening, overtly angry, aggressive, or severely troubled employee, and a referral for treatment made. Other referrals may be needed as well, to medical, employee assistance, grievance, security, or other supportive resources. Protective measures may also be taken.

Since initial data are usually very limited, the first opinions that are reached about risk of violence are likely to require additional information and the involvement of other resources or options in supporting the employee and de-escalating the situation. The process repeats itself over and over until the threat is resolved. The process looks like this:

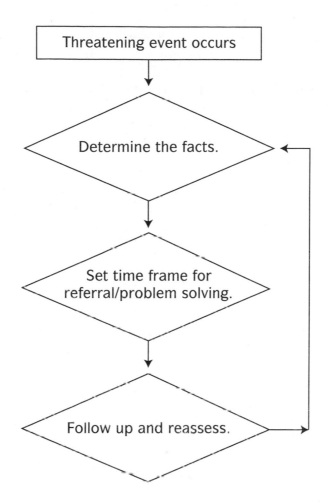

Along each step of fact-finding and problem solving, Monahan's ten questions (see Chapter 2) can help the violence response team reach a judgment about the employee's potential for violence:

1. What events precipitated the raising of the question of this person's potential for violence? In what context did these events take place? Am I clear about exactly what the person did to raise the concern of others? What context was it in? Do I have a clear description of what the aggressor did?

2. Do I have any information about the base rate of violence among individuals with this person's background?
3. What is the base rate of violent behavior among individuals of this person's background, as obtained from company incident reports and from shared industry data?
4. What are the sources of stress in the person's current environment? Are there a divorce, death in the family, or financial problems?
5. What cognitive or affective factors suggest that the person may be disposed to cope with stress in a violent manner? For example, underlying rage, poor cognitive skills, and substance abuse can make it difficult to problem solve effectively.
6. What cognitive or affective factors suggest that the person may be disposed to cope with stress in a nonviolent manner? For example, has the individual used the employee assistance program or filed grievances?
7. Who are the likely victims of the person's violence, and how accessible are they?
8. What means does the person have to commit violence?
9. What is the person's history of violent behavior?
10. How similar are the contexts in which the person has used violent coping mechanisms in the past to the contexts in which the person likely will function in the future?

Defusing a Potentially Violent Situation

No matter where you are in assessing or responding to potential violence, you must consistently manage your own feelings if you are to reach the nonviolent outcome you seek. Dominant among the emotions you may be feeling are frustration, anger, fear, and anxiety. You must stay calm and focused on your goal. In addition, you must deal with the employee in a calming manner.

When you are interviewing the employee in a particularly tense meeting, you may choose to switch from a confrontational setting to a semisocial one by serving refreshments and creating an informal, comfortable environment, as long as your behavior is not open to misinterpretation. Be careful to avoid seeming like an authority figure. Let the employee see you as a person, not as a symbol of the organization. Listen much more than you talk. Appear supportive, and show that you are trying to understand the situation from the employee's point of view. Don't justify, defend, or explain. Just listen, and try to understand.

The most common mistake people make in these situations is to focus on who is right and who is wrong. Don't try to determine blame, but merely seek to understand how the employee sees the problem. Try to tune into his experiences. Don't move to problem solving too quickly. You must first establish a sense of understanding, trust, and reduced tension. Let the person walk, pace, or move around in order to help dissipate his energy and anxiety. Offer to let the employee bring in a friend, co-worker, or supervisor whom he trusts for support if he wants to. Above all, do not issue ultimatums in either your words or through the tone of your voice. Instead, show concern and empathy, while you try to gather the facts from the employee's perspective.

Accept irrational attitudes and negative feelings without necessarily agreeing with them. Work at adding new bargaining positions or compromises to the person's view of possibilities. Before giving advice, find out what the person has tried or thought of to solve the problem. You can assume that the employee has thought about the situation and tried to resolve it somehow and that he is considering more ideas. Remember that the employee is the authority on his situation. Try to imagine as well as you can the position he is in and what his life situation is. Always be respectful and empowering. Don't be judgmental or self-righteous. The more respectful you are in giving advice, the more likely the person will be able to hear what you're saying. Be sensitive to whether the employee will be interested in your input. Maybe he is just looking for a sympathetic ear. Perhaps he is so hurt or afraid that he is unable to hear any ideas from anyone else. Check this before plowing ahead with good advice. If you are asked, you may want to share what has worked for you in a similar situation or how you would handle the situation under question, but avoid sounding condescending. After listening to the story, you can offer a tested solution without being pushy.

The employees or customers about whom you have concerns are likely to respond to hearing "no" to any request with extensive blaming and high levels of emotional intensity. They can accuse and severely distort and devalue the qualities of those with whom they are interacting. In their uproar, they can be irrational and oversensitive and can misinterpret other people's behavior. They will probably be suffering from severe anxiety, whether apparent or hidden.

Managing a Potentially Violent Incident

There may be times when you are attempting to assess a situation and find that your attempts at defusing it are not working. At such times, the biggest challenge you face is to stay calm and centered. If you lose your cool, you will probably become frustrated and provocative and intensify the level of stress. Instead, help the employee or customer to feel respected and heard and to see options. Defusing is a very important part of dealing with a person whose frustration is rising to the level of aggression. You want to make the situation less tense.

Dealing with high-risk employees whose behaviors are escalating should always include consideration of preventive actions that may be needed if the situation worsens. Don't hesitate to consult experts on difficult cases. When an employee is flagged as high risk or as in crisis, you may need to move to a different range of responses, including:

1. *Incapacitate the employee or customer whose behavior is escalating out of control.* You must negate his opportunity to act violently. Depending on the particular situation, there are a number of different strategies you can use—from making sure that the correct doors are locked to having the person incarcerated or involuntarily evaluated for hospitalization.

2. *See that the potential victim(s) of an employee or customer are made more difficult to harm (also known as target hardening).* If an

employee is talking about hurting a supervisor, she may need to be removed from the worksite or transferred to a different supervisor, just to be safe. If the person is out of the worksite on a leave of absence, security may need to be warned not to let the person into the building, and it may be necessary to monitor the person's ongoing condition. If an employee is threatening a particular individual, you may have a responsibility to see that the potential victim is warned of the danger and protected in whatever way possible, from seeking a restraining order to providing protection. Securing your facility or store is one way to accomplish this task. Another is having an evacuation plan in case of a violent act. During a shooting, whether by a robber or a disgruntled employee, is not the time for employees to figure out how to protect themselves.

3. *Intensify treatment.* When an employee's behavior appears to be escalating toward violence, more intense and attentive treatments may be necessary. Initiating the use of medications and increasing the frequency of treatment sessions can help someone who is on the edge of losing control. It is amazing how often the person will tell other people if she is not under control or is unable to work or to return to work in a safe way. Because the employee cannot be watched twenty-four hours a day unless he is hospitalized, you may need to involve a person he trusts to help get him to treatment and to monitor behavior between treatment sessions.

It is often very useful to obtain a second opinion. You and your team may have missed something. We all have our blind spots, particularly in the heat of a crisis. In addition, all events, conversations, and input from various parties involved in the situation should be fully and accurately documented, along with a rationale for the actions taken or not taken. These documents are helpful in reviewing situations that are not improving in order to consider additional options. It is very easy to overlook what ought to be the obvious and best solutions. These records will be useful if there is litigation down the road, as well. After the crisis is resolved, the completed forms can also be reviewed as you consider revisions in policy.

If a situation deteriorates, you may have to do some damage

control before it gets better. This can include quickly communicating with workers in your company. You should have a preset means of doing so. You may need to reach out to small or large groups of employees who are feeling intimidated, concerned, or frightened by the evolving situation. While you need to maintain the privacy of the employee involved in the incident, you also need to manage the reactions of his co-workers. It is important that panic not be allowed to set in.

When the situation is not being defused adequately, increase your level of awareness. Pay attention to the environment and to potential dangers and think about possible outside assistance. Consider initiating these steps immediately, even if you doubt that the person is about to become violent:

1. *Casually interrupt the interview to call and request something, while actually calling for help.* If your gut tells you the person is about to lose control, she probably is. You may have co-workers join you and explain in a nonthreatening way why you are doing so.

2. *Don't be a hero.* If you believe that the employee is capable of real harm, bring in security. Depending on the situation, this may be as subtle as having them within shouting distance or as overt as having them sit in the room during the conversation.

3. *Keep the employee or customer engaged in conversation about her feelings or a specific problem.* Silent periods can increase anxiety, so keep the conversation going. Pace it so that it does not become too controversial at any time. Don't speak too quickly, and be sure to keep your voice calm.

4. *Encourage the employee to be seated if at all possible.* While it can be helpful to allow an agitated employee to pace to relieve the tension, when she reaches the point where you fear she may explode, your focus should switch to your own protection. If she were suddenly to become violent, she would be easier to contain sitting down. You should remain seated as well.

5. *If the employee becomes more threatening, explain the consequences of violent behavior without condemnation, and remain calm.* This must be done in a noncombative but clear and reality-bound manner.

6. *Use your common sense, and don't let your emotions take over.*
I will never forget the story of a psychotic man who walked into
a hospital emergency room and told the attending psychiatrist
that voices were telling him to shoot a doctor. He also mentioned
that he had a gun in his pocket. The psychiatrist panicked and
became paralyzed with fear. Common sense should have told
him to flee, but fear prevented him from reacting. The man took
his silence as an indication that the voices were accurate, and he
shot the psychiatrist dead.

It is important that all staff involved in risk situations be
aware of the safety and security procedures that are in place.
There have been instances in which people with firearms walked
into companies where there was no method of notifying employees that someone was walking down the hall firing away. Safety
procedures, like fire evacuation plans and medical emergency
procedures, should be known and rehearsed. It is also important
that security personnel be readily available. Do you have an
agreement with the local police department to come if you call
them with a certain message? Do you know what they would
do when they arrived? In spite of your best preventive measures,
emergencies can happen; having these procedures talked
through ahead of time can save lives.

Phases of a Crisis

There are a number of things a company can do to prevent workplace violence. First, it must realize that violence is a real possibility. Then it must prepare properly by writing appropriate policies and training employees to report all threatening behavior
immediately. It must develop a violence response team trained
to assess employees and situations as risks arise and able to figure out the correct method of shoring up the employee's ability to
cope without resorting to violence. It must identify the resources,
both internal and external, that can help defuse the tension and
stress that often lead to violence.

These resources must also address the individual at whatever level of crisis she presents in order to be restabilized. The team must have the ability to creatively problem solve so that the employee and the company can both find viable options. Finally, there must be staff on hand to help her adjust after the crisis.

But in spite of its best efforts at prevention, a company may find itself with a crisis on its hands. Therefore, it is helpful to know a little about crises in general and the critical elements that go into dealing with them successfully. After all, a crisis does not occur in a vacuum; it results from a build-up of tensions and occurs over time. A crisis generally progresses in phases, and at each phase the person in crisis needs a different kind of help in order to de-escalate the growing tension. It is also well to remember that there are certain responses that, despite the best of intentions, are known to escalate the employee's tension, and possibly jeopardize the safety of the person trying to help as well.

This section describes the typical phases of escalation a person may go through once she is in crisis. It also discusses the responses that are most likely to defuse the crisis at each phase:[1]

1. *The anxiety phase.* Whatever has occurred to create the crisis, the employee is almost certainly feeling considerable anxiety. This anxiety must be responded to, because it is overwhelming and typically uppermost in the employee's mind. The response that is most needed is support. The focus of the response should be on the employee's feelings.

Four sets of skills are required to address the needs of the employee at this point. The first is the ability to tune in to where the employee is. This requires developing some empathy for what the person has been experiencing and what his perspective might be. The second involves building a working relationship with the employee and requires communication skills that allow the helper to understand and connect with the employee in crisis. The third skill is the ability to provide structure by clarifying the role of the helper, the employee's expectations, and the pur-

---

[1] Adapted from "Nonviolent Crisis Intervention," National Crisis Prevention Institute, Inc. (Brookfield, Wisconsin © 1984).

pose and likely duration of the interview. The fourth skill is active listening. This is a technique to help the employee feel accepted and understood and to have the opportunity to vent his feelings verbally rather than physically.

2. *The defensive phase.* As the employee comes to feel more and more trapped without viable options, he is likely to become quite defensive. The response that is needed is a directive one. The employee is getting into serious difficulty and needs to be shown how to get out. The focus of the conversations should be on both the employee's feelings and his behaviors.

There are four sets of skills necessary to deal with this phase of the crisis. As the employee becomes more tense and ominous, the other person must have great self-control. This requires being able to manage your own feelings as the crisis escalates, to stay calm, and to retain good judgment. The second skill is the ability to manage the employee's anger. No easy task, this includes being able to explore the angry feelings, defuse or disarm them, and redirect the anger to productive channels. The third skill is the effective use of body language, observing that of the employee and communicating nonverbally in such a way as to reduce the threat and retain control of the situation.

In meetings characterized by high levels of tension and stress, it is particularly important to use body language to pacify the situation. A physically calm appearance—with palms unclenched, with relaxed facial muscles, and with eyes focused directly at the employee without fear or anger—sends an important message to the employee in distress and helps to calm him down.

By the same token, if the employee's tension and anxiety begin to escalate during the meeting, the increasing risk for an explosion may be communicated more clearly by body language than by words. Increased perspiration, squirming, shortness of breath, and tightened fists can indicate that he is losing control.

The fourth skill is the ability to set limits, including being able to provide feedback about what is acceptable and unacceptable behavior in a way that helps the employee to develop more self-control.

3. *The acting-out phase.* This is the phase in which the em-

ployee has lost some of his control. The response that is needed is professional control and containment. The focus is on the employee's behavior.

It is necessary to recognize the behavioral signs of imminent violence and to terminate, reschedule, or restructure the interview to ensure the safety of all involved. It is also necessary to be able to protect oneself without bringing on retaliation or harm to the employee.

4. *The tension-reduction phase.* At some point during the crisis, the employee will be ready to accept help in reducing his level of tension. The response needed is a therapeutic-type rapport that is caring, helpful, understanding, and, most important, calm. The focus is on the employee's feelings and behavior.

The skills needed in this phase are, again, the ability to tune in to the employee, to identify with how the employee might be feeling about his behavior, to communicate effectively in order to understand and reconnect with the employee, and to listen actively so that the employee can express his feelings and understand what occurred. It should be obvious that once an employee's behavior has escalated to the point of crisis, much of what goes on is beyond what a company is capable of coping with. That is why appropriate referral along the way to capable external resources is so important.

It is critical during a crisis to maintain your emotional control and to handle your own fear and anxiety. Anxiety is a natural, protective response to a threat. Unfortunately, it can be infectious. Professionals who encounter it during a crisis need to recognize and acknowledge their own anxiety, understand the sources of it, and master techniques to control it. Usually, the reaction to a threat is defensive: either fight or flight. Becoming aware of the sources of your own anxiety and controlling your physical responses to it are vital to remaining in control of a crisis. Are you aware of your own physical cues to anxiety? Some of the symptoms of anxiety can be: sweaty palms, rapid speech, shortness of breath, heart palpitations, a sense of panic and intense fear, a feeling of being distracted, difficulty concentrating, shaky hands, clumsiness, stuttering, muscle tension in the shoulders or neck or other areas of the body, nausea, dry mouth, intestinal distress, and physical pains.

Stress is an inevitable result of being confronted by a situation that is scary and threatening. One source of stress is your own personal emotional vulnerabilities. You need to know your emotional "hot buttons" and to develop strategies to keep them out of risk situations. You need to desensitize yourself from being vulnerable to provocation. Identify the most offensive thing an employee could say or do and develop coping techniques for handling it. Find a co-worker to practice and support you in rehearsing your responses.

Another source of stress is a lack of confidence in your ability to handle the situation. It is important that you have a realistic sense of your strengths and weaknesses in handling highly conflicted and tense people. No one comes by these skills naturally, although some people are better at it than others. Everyone on a violence response team needs to have training in how to deal with a crisis and to practice and develop skills.

Because stress can easily build up as you are trying to manage a crisis, it is critical that you be aware of your own limits, recognize the signs of burnout, and know when to attend to your needs for leisure, socialization, rest, or pleasure—and to ask for help. Learning physiological control or stress management techniques can be a crucial aid in managing your own stress. There are four forms: deep breathing, progressive muscle relaxation, visualization, and meditation. Each can help you maintain yourself in a calm and steady way and communicate this calm to the employee with whom you are working. What does your voice sound like? What are your facial expressions? As much as possible, your expression should be neutral, nonprovocative, and nonstimulating. Keep your voice calm and relaxing.

It is important to have a clear and specific knowledge of your company's policies and procedures in handling crises. It makes a big difference if you believe that the company really values employee safety. To get through a crisis, the employee trying to handle the crisis must have sufficient external resources to fall back on. There must also be internal supports, best found in the form of the violence response team.

The Forgotten Step: Dealing With the Aftermath

When the employee has been assessed and the escalation broken, when life appears to be getting back to normal, it's easy to think that the crisis is over. In fact, after a frightening threat or near-violent occurrence, the company must still deal with the resulting employee grief, trauma, and personal loss. The indirect costs accompanying even incidents that do not go beyond the verbal phase may be significant and may include a decline in employee morale and lower productivity. Companies would be wise to take steps to limit the potentially devastating aftereffects that can result from threats and incidences of violence at work. Just because a potentially violent employee is off the job does not mean that those who have experienced her threatening behavior have been able to forget about what happened.

There are four tasks still to be accomplished after a threat or incident is handled and resolved that will impact the residual costs on the company to a considerable degree. The first task is to review what happened in order to improve future prevention strategies. The second is to evaluate what has been learned. The third is to take care of yourself in light of the effects the tensions have had on you. It is far too common for people to deny their own needs. The fourth task is to take care of other employees who may have been affected by exposure to violence. Tasks 3 and 4 are far too often forgotten.

Trauma can result from threats or actual acts of violence, regardless of their source. A threat of a shooting or an interaction with a very tense and threatening employee can affect a company environment almost as much as if there had been an actual violent event. Much has been written about trauma after such events as explosions, hijackings, airplane crashes, and violent acts on the job. What these have in common is that they have a major impact on the lives and well-being of the public; involve a product, service, or facility; generate widespread publicity; and may place the organization at fault. A disaster affects different sectors of a company in different ways, depending on whether they are executives, involved staff groups, or employees in general. It triggers a host of individual, group, and organizational psychological effects. There are strong emotional reactions from victims and their families, the media, the legal community, the public at large, and, in some cases, the government. These reactions force the company to take remedial action involving its operations, products or service, and facility; to defend itself; and to deal with employee relations. It is typical for employees and the public to blame the company after a tragedy.

After trauma, people often avoid things associated with the traumatic event and experience a numbing of general responsiveness. They may relive the traumatic event repeatedly and feel a need to be extra-vigilant. This reaction can take a terrible toll on productivity and effectiveness, as well as on the well-being of employees. Healing requires that trauma be taken seriously and that people be trained to recognize the signs of stress and depression early on. It is important to provide interventions immediately after an incident. It can't be business as usual. You must respond to employees in tangible and believable ways and help them talk out their reactions, or they will act it out in their behaviors.

There are now psychological firms that specialize in postincidence debriefing. The day after an event such as a shooting, they gather those who witnessed the incident to talk about their reactions. The goals of the first debriefing session, while people are still in shock, are to let participants know that their reactions are normal and to provide a phone number where they can receive support if they need it. An important aspect of the effort is helping the employees understand that their reactions are not unique so that they do not feel isolated. The longer an individual suppresses her traumatic feelings, the greater the danger of flashbacks, depression, hypervigilance, fear of the workplace, and other traumatic reactions. Both the Caplan studies of the survivors of the terrible fire at the Coconut Grove nightclub in Boston, the beginning of all trauma research, and the more recent Veterans Hospital studies of soldiers who served in Vietnam have shown that individuals who do not acknowledge their reactions to a trauma can develop posttraumatic stress disorders that can go on for a lifetime if not treated.

The best way to prevent trauma-related stress disorders is to let people talk in groups about what happened and about their emotional reactions to their experience after the shock has died down. They should be encouraged to remember the details, from their first thoughts to their final feelings and reactions. They should discuss symptoms that they may be experiencing, such as changes in eating or sleeping patterns, feelings of depression or anxiety, and interpersonal problems. They should be educated about typical trauma reactions and taught how to take care of themselves. The object of such programs is to let people know their feelings are normal and to get them to talk about them, rather than allow them to become destructive forces in their emotional lives.

Failure to resolve traumatic events often takes the form of physical reactions (changes in health, headaches, gastrointestinal problems, sleep disturbances, fatigue); emotional problems (fear or paranoia, guilt, anxiety, depression, irritability, helplessness, overintensity); problems in thinking (overfocusing on an event, confusion, reduced attention span, difficulty with decision making, hypervigilance, poor memory); and behavior changes (nightmares, isolation, crying, and avoidance).

To take care of yourself after surviving a traumatic threat or event, you need to get vigorous physical exercise within twenty-four hours, get plenty of rest, eat well, maintain a normal schedule, avoid boredom, socialize, have contact with friends, talk about what you've been through, accept dreams and flashbacks, and organize and attend an incident stress session to debrief.

Chapter 8

Leadership and Organizational Dynamics

An article called "Let the Good Times Roll—And a Few More Heads," which appeared in the January 31, 1994, issue of *Business Week* magazine, does a very nice job of characterizing what is happening to the economy. Whether you are a corporate leader or an employee in the United States, Japan, or Germany, this is the situation you face:

> Funny thing. U.S. economic growth is expanding at a considerable clip. . . . Yet some of the best and brightest among America's big corporations are continuing to restructure. In the year's first fortnight, such stalwart—and profitable—outfits as Gillette, Eli Lilly, and Arco have announced significant layoffs and financial changes. More are coming: Insurance giant Aetna Life & Casualty Co. is expected to detail a major restructuring within weeks. Even in technology sectors where the U.S. is a clear world leader, big companies are cutting back. In addition to GTE, Pacific Bell, Xerox, Electronic Data Systems, and American Telephone and Telegraph are all hacking away. What's going on? Simply put, executives are nervous. They hear increasing demands for greater value from customers, and feel the relentless pressure of global competition and fundamental shifts in technology. Haunting nearly everyone is the memory of those that have stumbled—IBM and General Motors, among others—and the well-publicized dismissals of CEOs who didn't act quickly enough.

The fundamentals of business around the globe have changed. Companies everywhere are being forced to change their ways of dealing with employees from the top to the bottom of the organization, and with their customers as well. More and more is expected of fewer and fewer. Companies that have temporarily improved their earnings by lowering their head count continue to face severe long-term pressures in their marketplaces. Global competition is ferocious. Many corporate boards of directors are becoming more demanding. At every level of the organization, employees are being asked to take on more complex and demanding sets of tasks. In almost every case, the demands include cost cutting, improved efficiency, innovation, and strategic thinking. While some people thrive in this changing environment, many people are becoming its casualties.

Unfortunately, employees affected by the constant changes and increasing demands of today's high-pressure business environment are ever more likely to become aggressive in the workplace. Mounting work-related stress combined with perceived or real lack of job security increase worker anxiety and volatility. General corporate policy and culture can play key roles in establishing an environment within which violence is discouraged. To decrease effectively the likelihood of a violent event, companies need to anticipate the stress caused by their dynamics and culture and to implement comprehensive prevention programs.

For any program to be truly successful, however, it is essential that upper management actively steer and support the effort. Many corporate leaders are, in fact, beginning to become concerned about workplace violence, if only in the interest of their company's profitability. A dysfunctional workplace is not a productive one. One of the largest organizations to take on the issue of preventing workplace violence, and one from which other companies can learn, is the U.S. Postal Service.

What Your Company Can Learn
From the Postal Service

Since 1983, thirty-four people have been killed and twenty wounded in post-office–related shootings. Investigators have said that work tensions or unstable employees were a factor in every case. The Postal Service hopes that by overhauling its hiring practices, it can avoid employing troubled individuals like the former Royal Oak, Michigan, worker who killed four supervisors and himself in 1991. As part of a postmortem of the event, investigators learned that he had a reputation for violent outbursts while in the military and had a less-than-honorable discharge. They are now using an outside firm to check applicants' military, criminal, employment, and driving records. They are also carefully evaluating job candidates' performance in interviews and on civil service tests. Many current employees fear that studying the problem of violence will lead to profiling potential perpetrators and that this in turn could result in discrimination against Vietnam veterans who have found employment in the Postal Service.

The Postal Service is also trying to rid itself of its paramilitary management practices and to free itself of its authoritarian, hierarchical culture. Like those at General Electric, future employee and manager performance evaluations will include the opinions of subordinates in addition to those of supervisors. The human relations skills measured in such evaluations will be used to determine which managers will be promoted; those with poor human relations skills will stay where they are and receive additional training.

Much has been written about the problems of violence in the U.S. Postal Service. Its paramilitary culture and hostile labor relations are seen by many as contributing to the high number of homicides within the organization. It is easy to see how a top-down, highly authoritarian environment increases rebelliousness, polarizes work environments, and creates a breeding ground for violence. It is easier in such a context for an employee to view violence as an acceptable response to being wronged or mistreated by supervisors she does not trust, to policies that are unfair, and to grievance procedures that are rigged. Given these perceptions, it becomes easier for the employee to decide that the only alternative is for her to take matters into her own hands. Picking up a weapon becomes the only viable option, in the employee's view.

In spite of all the publicity, it may not be true that the Postal

Service actually has a higher rate of workplace violence than business in general. The statistics indicate that it had .63 homicides per 100,000 workers from 1980 to 1986, compared with an overall rate for industry of .71 per 100,000. Nonetheless, because of the enormous amount of negative publicity it has received as a result of the problem, the Postal Service leadership has been looking for ways to lower the incidence of violence at its facilities. Other companies can learn from what it is doing.

The Post Office has had an authoritarian culture that included an individual merit system, rigid rules and regulations, and an exclusively top-down management style. Management led all efforts in an arbitrary manner, and there was low worker involvement. In contrast, the Postal Service is now trying to use climate surveys, training programs, and 360-degree feedback in which supervisors, co-workers, and subordinates are asked for feedback in order to move toward a participative culture. It is trying to empower groups and to make them accountable for their own activities and is moving to a group merit system, using stricter prehire criteria, and developing a quicker and more humane termination process. Its new crisis intervention policy states that any threatening remark or gesture is unacceptable, that there will be no tolerance for violence or the threat of violence, that all threats will be thoroughly investigated, and that individuals engaging in unacceptable activity will be subject to discipline and possible removal.

Preparedness and Prevention: How the Post Office Is Dealing With Violence

Besides reevaluating its hiring procedures and its corporate culture, the Postal Service is taking five initiatives to prevent additional occurrences of violence.

1. It has developed a crisis intervention assessment plan to establish protocols for assessing threats and their potential for violence. The plan's purpose is to minimize the possibility that a threatening situation will escalate into a crisis that could lead to violence. Key elements of the plan are the identification of warning signs of potential violence and the training of supervi-

sors in how to use them. The plan will be used to teach staff to do threat assessments by evaluating an employee's tone of voice and ability to carry out a threat, investigating the triggering event that caused the employee to react, understanding the context in which the incident occurred, and watching for the behavior that emerges after the event is confronted.

2. A critical incident team (a violence response team) will receive training in the early warning signs of violence; fact gathering; the stages of violent interactions; trauma; de-escalation of potential violence; the uses of role playing; privacy issues; legal issues; labor relations issues; and "care-fronting," the Postal Service term for "confronting."

3. Training areas for all supervisors and managers will include stress management, effective communication, team building, conflict resolution, change management, dealing with difficult employees, terminations, accommodations, effective listening, security, self-discipline and emotional control, dealing with customers, building a high-performance team, and telephone skills. Line supervisors are being trained in front-line intervention.

If you recall the model of how individuals spiral into violence (see Chapter 2), you will see that many of the educational programs the Postal Service is introducing are designed to enhance the coping skills of the employee and of the supervisor or manager. If stress is the subjective experience of feeling unable to respond to the demands of the world around you, developing better skills for working with people and handling the tasks of the job should lower the employee's stress level and enhance his sense of capability.

4. The Postal Service is collecting data relating to violence prevention, including personnel records, medical records, reports from fellow employees and superiors, and outside data. This strategy is part of getting to know its employees better and tracking volatile individuals more effectively.

5. The Postal Service is providing training for its senior managers, one of the most frequently overlooked aspects of corporate violence prevention. If the executive staff does not understand the issues involved in workplace violence and genuinely

support the preventive measures being taken, the efforts will not work very well. Senior staff needs to receive an overview of the training on violence that is being offered to the rest of the company. It also needs to understand that early warning signs for violence exist and how they should be used; the role of the violence response team and its arrangement of internal and external resources that support violence prevention; and, above all, how the organizational culture and the company's leadership style affect both the success of the business and factors associated with workplace violence. By focusing on these issues, senior management can identify and improve many of the human factor issues involved in improving its productivity, quality, and customer service while taking measures to prevent workplace violence.

The Postal Service has come to see the connections that link training its supervisors to deal with emotionally charged employees, increasing employee human relations effectiveness, giving clear career track guidelines that are related to relationship competencies, teaching stress management and human effectiveness habits, building teams, and helping leaders and potential leaders to prevent and deal with workplace violence.

Corporate Culture and the High-Pressure Workplace

The Postal Service has put into place policies designed to create a dramatic turnaround in its management style—a style that has in the past led to strikes and other forms of labor-management struggles. Corporations as well as other public bureaucracies suffer from similar problems. Perhaps workplace violence will be the wake-up call that alerts companies to the fact that they must develop modern business practices. The fact is that leadership styles can either mitigate or exacerbate the possibility of workplace violence. Most executives have not yet fully comprehended that horizontal organizations need to be led in an entirely different way from hierarchical ones. They have not grasped at a gut level what employee empowerment means.

The Changing Employee Contract:
The Stress of Continuous Improvement

The changes in the employer/employee relationship since the 1970s and early 1980s have been widely discussed and written about. Many people are struggling with what these changes mean and are reacting in intensely emotional and personal ways. These changes are the source of great anxiety. Outsourcing, restructuring, outtasking, and plant and office relocation are foul words to many. In the context of these kinds of changes, company leaders must set by word and example a tone that creates a positive work environment in which people feel heard and respected. What is needed is a leadership style and qualities like those found in a fully participatory work environment. When respect, accountability, and open communication prevail, preventing violence by reducing tension offers the dual benefits of developing a more effective workforce and preventing violence at the same time.

Job stress, a result of burnout on the job and of increased competition for fewer jobs, can be both a cause and an effect of workplace violence. Job stress increases as more workers compete for fewer jobs. People feel more pressure to work harder and are more intensely aware of the risks of failing. The Northwestern National Life Insurance Institute for Occupational Safety and Health found that 37 percent of workers said they expected to burn out in their current job within the next two years. Highly stressed workers experience twice the threat of violence and harassment compared to employees who experience lower levels of stress. They are also more likely to turn to substance abuse than are those not under pressure, which carries its own potential for violence.

The factors that enable some employees to thrive on challenge and change and to rise to the occasion, and others to feel anxious and overwhelmed, are purely subjective. I have said that how a person experiences the world around him is critical to whether that person becomes violent. This subjective experience is based on a number of factors, not the least of which are how the person thinks about and emotionally reacts to what is happening.

People who feel in control, who feel up to the task, and who have a positive view of their own capabilities will take challenge as an opportunity. Those with a less optimistic emotional temperament or who have recently experienced defeats that have threatened their self-esteem may experience similar challenges as stressful or even overwhelming. Whether they respond in a positive or negative way has a great deal to do with where they experience the locus of control, whether it feels like an adult-child relationship or an adult-adult relationship, if there are sadistic elements to it, and what the alternatives are for resolving conflicts.

The fundamental contract between employees and employers has changed. Because of new business needs and circumstances, employment no longer carries a sense of security and stability. Historically, careers have been lifelong relationships between the worker and the company. With the corporate mergers of the 1980s and the massive layoffs that resulted from the economic recession of the early 1990s, individuals are being asked to produce more in shorter periods of time, often for the same or less pay than they were receiving. In some of these high-stress situations, employees can feel hopeless about their economic prospects, overwhelmed by the employer's demands and expectations, and discouraged by the downsizings and mergers that take away career opportunities.

Employees: Assets, Expenses, or People

Companies used to think of employees as assets to be developed. Since the early 1980s, they have been thinking of employees as costs to be reduced. Building up used to be the corporate goal. Now smaller is better. Managers used to think of themselves as nurturing the skills of subordinates. Now they think of themselves as buyers and sellers of commodities—people who possess certain skill sets. In this context, it becomes even more important for a company that is going to terminate or dramatically change workers' employment statuses to learn to do it the right way. The key ingredient is to treat people with respect and dignity and to overexplain what is happening with a clear and honest business rationale.

One particular group in the workforce may be feeling the stress of what's happening to corporate America more than others. These employees were hired in the 1960s when jobs were readily available, even for people with minimum skills. Most have been with their current employers for long periods of time, maybe twenty-five years or more. Now, all of a sudden, they find that they are considered by their employers to be dead weight. They may be people who were always on the poor side of performance on their jobs but who never created any problems, either, or they may have performed adequately over the years but find that, with rising expectations and increased scrutiny, their companies are not willing to keep them. They have become dependent on a certain level of income to support their standard of living. They may carry heavy debt. They see no career options and nowhere to turn for a viable replacement for their current jobs.

Here is one real-life example:[1] A human resources professional described the situation: "These people become panicked when faced with the loss of a job. They need to be handled very sensitively." For example, an employer managed to salvage a less-than-ideal employee who fit this pattern. John had been getting adequate reviews for years because his supervisor didn't want to deal with his unsatisfactory performance. After a merger, the company culture changed, and employees were expected to do more. John was given a performance appraisal that threw him into an absolute panic. The review was so potentially sensitive that the supervisor's boss and the human resources manager both decided to attend to lend some objectivity to the event. "He was very controlled but totally devastated by the criticism," said the HR manager, who asked that the company name not be used. He was told that the people he had to work with found him intimidating. "Perhaps they know I've been trained to kill," he said. Then he began to attack the supervisor verbally, calling him an alcoholic and saying he knew what that was like because of his father's alcoholism. According to the HR manager,

---

[1] Linda Thurnburg, "Difficult Employees Need Special Attention," *HRMagazine* (July 1993).

"We told him to take the review with him and think about it, and that we would get him on an improvement program. We didn't specify any date by which his performance needed to improve, and we didn't make any threats. We just said you need to get up to speed in certain areas. On Monday, he called the office, sobbing and hysterical. He told a secretary they had taken away his manhood. On Tuesday, I called and was told he was at the doctor's office. On Wednesday, I got a call from the local hospital claims department. He was in the psychiatric unit."

John had severe anxiety; he couldn't face the people whom he perceived as having insulted him so badly. After his psychiatrist said he could come back to work, he was expected twice and didn't show up. Later he called and spoke to the HR manager. "I can't come to work because I wouldn't be able to back down from those people; I'd have to hurt somebody," he said.

The fact is that work is important to most people more than as just a source of income. As societal supports have dwindled and institutions have lost relevance, many employees have come to depend on their worksites for social and emotional support. They look at their jobs as a place where they belong, a source of meaning and value, and a way to define who they are. The more a person is tied into his company in these ways, the more vulnerable he is to becoming violent if he experiences loss or degradation on the job. Employees need help to learn not to base all of their self-esteem on their work. The business climate of the 1990s, in which employers demand more and more of employees, leads some employees to sacrifice almost everything else in their lives for their work. This can set up employees to become so overinvested in work that when the now inevitable changes in their employment do occur, they experience them as overwhelming stress, leaving them at great risk for harming themselves or others. Senior managers need to prevent or limit this phenomenon by encouraging and supporting employees to have a balanced life that includes other relationships, emotional connections, and commitments beyond work that give their lives meaning and worth.

Diversity: Opportunity and Challenge

Diversity represents a major business opportunity for most companies. Having a more culturally, racially, and gender-diverse workforce will allow them to understand new and growing markets, as well as stimulating new ways of thinking and of accomplishing the job because of the additional inputs and perspectives diversity creates. On the other hand, negative reactions to increased diversity in the workforce may also become a major source of workplace violence in the future. Racism and discrimination in a multicultural, multiethnic work environment can result in hostility between groups that exacerbates competition over jobs and promotions and creates a perception of bias and unfairness.

The same types of tensions that already occur among various ethnic and racial groups in society at large can be expected to enter the corporate environment as the workforce becomes more diversified. Businesses must root out the overt and the subtle forms of racism and sexism. Diversity issues are especially susceptible to being compounded severely by a lack of effective management practices, and the situations in which cultural biases are likely to surface may be especially susceptible to toxic supervisors, whose own prejudices or needs for power make existing tensions worse. Escalation toward violence is typically not one person's fault but the result of many people's interactions. There must be clear statements from senior management that discrimination is not acceptable and will not be tolerated within the company. Personnel policies should spell out the consequences of both overt and subtle prejudiced behavior. Diversity training and education can help to deal with these issues directly in a way that de-escalates tensions.

The New Demands on Corporate Leaders

An increasingly unrestrained global marketplace is generating a greatly intensified competitive environment for most companies. In addition to creating fundamental and dramatic changes in the employer-employee relationship, these new pressures are putting new and complex demands on the leaders of those organizations. Leading and managing a company is much more complicated than it used to be, because markets and competitors can now shift very rapidly and sometimes unpredictably. Those who are responsible for running corporations have more and more data with which to analyze and less and less certainty with which to determine directions that will ensure the future success and viability of their businesses.

In addition, the new, flat, nonpyramidal, "horizontal" organizational structure that is required to enable companies to respond quickly to customers and to changing markets demands a leadership style profoundly different, in many ways, from the old pyramidal structure.

All of these demands seem to point toward the ideal of participatory management, which may be one of the great buzzwords of our day, taking on such a vague and inclusive meaning as to become meaningless. The concept of participatory management has been around for a while, but as companies avail themselves of the new levels of technology that allow the deletion of middle layers of management, and as continuous quality improvement efforts keep finding that worker involvement and initiative are critical to success, the concept is taking on new relevance and timeliness. Participatory management involves employees and supervisors in decision making. It values listening to employees and treating them with respect. It creates adult-to-adult relationships in which trust is built on mutual respect, mutual need, and shared goals and values. Participatory management means moving away from power relationships of one-up–one-down to empowering and open communication. In fact, a participatory management style requires the development of many of the organizational dynamics that are also involved in preventing workplace violence at the organizational level.

It takes real courage for senior managers to let others in on their uncertainty and doubts. Many leaders feel that they must take public positions to convince stockholders and employees that the ship is well in hand. The reality is that employees are all too familiar with the current uncertainties of the business landscape. Sharing reality with employees in a human and honest way may allow others to take potshots at management, but it also opens the way for top managers to discover the magical quality of leadership that will allow them to venture into new worlds with the kind of employee following that is no longer attainable from the now antiquated concept of "just be loyal, work hard, and we'll take care of you."

The same issues involved in leading a company's workforce apply to dealing effectively with customers, as well. Customers need to be viewed as business partners, on the basis not of the old notion of loyalty but of the new reality of mutual interest. Listening closely and responding affirmatively and with understanding to a customer's needs are the best ways to prevent violence from them. It is also the best way to make the sale or develop repeat business. If customer dissatisfaction is the cause of 19 percent of all workplace violence, it is essential that companies learn to create win-win situations with their customers. It also makes great business sense.

The Role of the Corporate Leader in Preventing Workplace Violence

To prevent violence in their companies, company leaders must do more than just budget a violence response team and approve preventive policies and procedures. The leadership of a company can generate a mission and values statement that supports the way the company wants to treat people and the culture within which people want to work. By making the mission more than just words, corporate executives can show through example how to make this statement a reality. Ultimately, the best strategy for preventing workplace violence is to develop the right corporate culture, one that eschews power and authority in favor of:

- Respect
- Open communication and responsiveness
- Effective supervision
- Employee involvement, together with participation and development.

There are four steps senior executives must take to improve their company's business success and to prevent violence:

1. Create a positive organizational environment.
2. Get to know employees and avoid the dangerous consequences of the isolation of the corporate office.
3. Personally take precautions, set the tone, and think ahead.
4. Be proactive in managing change.

Create a Positive Organizational Environment

Make your company one where people feel heard and respected and where underlying feelings such as hurt and fear are acknowledged and attended to. Critical tasks such as early identification of and intervention in high-risk situations fall on supervisors and managers. Their ability to accomplish these tasks is, to a considerable degree, determined by the context in which they function. Another term for this context is *corporate culture,* and it is created by senior management.

Professor Edgar Schein of the Massachusetts Institute of Technology's Sloan School of Management has written extensively about corporate cultures and the evolution of a business environment from authoritarian to collaborative. He identifies four critical areas to consider in evaluating a company's culture: openness to conflict resolution; critical historical incidents or events in the life of the company; decisions on which manager actions to reward; and the role models presented by the executives. Each is a potential problem area that can contribute to the occurrence of violent events.

Another view of the same set of issues is from John P. Kotter and James L. Heskett, who describe how a stable, top-down culture founded on success can create a cultural myth of omniscience, rectitude, morality, boundless talent, and success as a birthright. Such a belief system can create a company where top executives fail to investigate issues, develop strategic or legal safeguards, take employee relations initiatives, or pay attention to public image. This stance can lead senior management to see potential change agents as enemies. Managers may demand compliance and vigilance from employees and seek scapegoats for problems, rather than identifying solutions for problems and conflicts as they arise. They may seek to decrease external contacts, including those with employees and their families, and avoid or minimize discussion of complaints.

In turn, this isolation and lack of responsiveness raises employee stress levels, triggering all kinds of emotional reactions, including guilt, high levels of anxiety or vigilance, and anger. The anxiety tends to narrow cognitive focus and thus to limit management's ability to see alternatives and options. It also triggers habitual and repetitive behaviors that may be less constructive than new ways of responding to problems or challenges.

This kind of inward, unrealistic, and ultimately dooming cultural mythology can arise when a company fails to hire enough top managers from outside the company to refocus the senior management group. I have seen companies that have slowly and quietly slid into this kind of culture. The biggest problem it brings is that it occurs without senior management's even being aware of what is happening to them.

Against these pressures, the chief executive plays a critical role in shaping the company's environment. She can do one of four things:

1. Become the voice of reason and strategic direction.
2. Provide a constructive and challenging role model.
3. Fall victim to group pressure and reinforce the downward spiral.
4. Become quick to anger and blame, and exacerbate the high risk of provocation and violence in the company.

Many employees don't realize the high degree of job stress that senior executives are now experiencing in the face of increased global competition and rapid changes in marketplaces and product mixes. These phenomena add more tension to corporate environments and affect the ways that executives react to fear and anxiety when they see them in their employees. When managers feel great pressure to produce significant results every quarter in the face of increasingly serious impediments, they may not have much patience to deal with the emotional condition of their workforce. The irony is that employees' state of mind may be a critical part of what makes or breaks the company's success for the quarter.

Because of the intense pressure to correct any downturn in profitability, companies are increasingly turning to senior executives who can turn results around quickly. I have seen company after company where very bright, short-term thinkers produced great results. These leaders, however, tend not to be the kind of senior managers who grasp, at a personal level, the issues involved in violence prevention and in establishing the most productive corporate culture for the long term. Given this dichotomy of skills, many chief executives face a choice between two types of subordinates to whom they can entrust the running of their organizations. The more tempting type may be the turnaround artist or short-term thinker who has an individualistic and immediate bottom-line approach. This person tends to be very bright, to have many great ideas, and to be gung-ho about moving forward immediately. In contrast, the second type of leader tends to be more an organizational creature, less oriented toward change but with a greater appreciation of the human element and the value of relationships within the company and with customers. Whichever type a senior executive chooses, she must be prepared to compensate for the individual manager's shortcomings as they affect the organization. Corporate culture is always the responsibility of the senior leadership. It is one of the two critical functions of corporate leadership (the other is defining the business strategy that will win in the company's marketplace).

Human resources executives and other company leaders often get so caught up in the rapid change and company reorganizations demanded by current business conditions that they forget to look at the human consequences of the changes they are shaping. Eighty percent of mergers eventually fail because companies don't deal well with the human factors that are involved, including individual employees' feelings and reactions to the merger and the unavoidable changes. Employees who are traumatized by changes in the workplace, such as acquisitions, mergers, significant senior management shakeups, and threatened downsizings, may suddenly question the meaning of their work lives, suffer a range of loss-related symptoms (e.g., shock, denial, anger, defensiveness, guilt, doubt, depression, and anxiety), and even exhibit post-traumatic stress symptoms (e.g., poor concentration, replaying events, and hypervigilance). These can lead to psychological or physical withdrawal. Each level of increasing stress has the potential to provoke some individuals to react violently.

Get to Know Your Employees

An antidote to the dangerous phenomenon of management isolation described by Kotter and Heskett is for company leaders to get to know and to listen to their employees. With all the potential trauma generated by the dramatic changes in the workplace of the 1990s, executives need to monitor employee stress levels and to provide potential releases. At the same time, they need to reverse the tendency to isolate themselves from outsiders, from employees, and from family and friends. Their genuine sharing with employees of their own reactions to difficult business situations can help subordinates cope with their own pressures and increase respect for the company's leaders. It establishes a climate of honesty in which managers can observe employees and their families for distress.

As everyone is asked to do more with fewer employees, knowing their staffs allows managers to evaluate staffing levels against a manageable level of demands, to require overly stressed managers to take time off before they make errors with their staff, and to reward efforts in meaningful ways. These actions create a productive and safe environment. They also allow senior managers to monitor conflict or stress within the larger work environment. It is this bigger context within which individual potentially violent situations escalate or are dealt with successfully.

Other methods by which senior executives can influence their company cultures in positive ways include providing frequent bulletins about developing situations, allowing employees to have direct contact with key executives, and communicating the reality and the likely consequences of such business events as profit declines, withdrawals from a line of business, layoffs, or reassignments. Employees typically feel helpless to affect changing business conditions and decisions, even when they are part of making the decisions, and it is easier for them to feel targeted, misunderstood, or treated unfairly when they are isolated from senior management. This isolation allows an us-versus-them chasm to develop. When dramatic workplace changes are occurring, employees need information about the responsibilities expected of them and the remedies they can take to adapt. They need permission to feel what they really feel in reaction. Senior managers need to allow this for themselves, too. They can begin by listening to employees and to each other. A company's leaders need to show employees by example that it is okay to verbalize their concerns. This requires a climate that allows individuals and groups to air these tensions. Enabling employees to express their feelings will create a wiser and stronger company, minimize long-term problems, and allow more informed and considered decision making about business issues.

If grievance and change systems are in place and are seen as timely and fair, then senior management dialogues and interactions can be used to build credibility, because they will be believable. The company becomes a supportive, realistic, and development-oriented environment, not a punitive one, and senior managers avoid the isolation and disconnections that are fatal to a company's success.

Personally Take Precautions, Set the Tone, and Think Ahead

It is not sufficient for corporate leaders to delegate to subordinates the development and implementation of a violence prevention program. Senior management must ensure that the company has taken appropriate actions to address the major contributors to potential violence in their organizations. They must also set the appropriate accompanying tone by their own words and behavior.

There are four major organizational contributors to workplace violence that must be monitored by the company's senior team. They include:

1. Poorly trained supervisors who trigger or reinforce intimidating behavior.
2. Authoritarian company cultures that deprive employees of dignity and respect and stifle positive responses to threats.
3. Downsizing and terminations that threaten an employee's sense of identity. Many people derive their main sense of who they are primarily from their jobs. Letting someone go, whatever the reason, must be done in such a way as to maintain the person's sense of dignity, without making her feel like a failure.
4. A failure to set policies that define clearly what behavior is unacceptable and that guide responses to harassment or intimidation. Such policies are necessary if unacceptable behavior is to be confronted before it can escalate.

Preventive elements must be in place and supported actively throughout an organization by its senior leadership. The role and responsibilities of upper management in successfully preventing and dealing with violence are as follows:

1. Mandate and train managers, supervisors, and employees to report all threatening behavior to an appropriate resource for investigation and response.
   - Open a communication line bypassing supervisors; include confidential channels.
   - Teach employees to recognize signs indicating that an employee may need help.
   - Communicate clear rules about violence, threats, intimidation, harassment, and weapons, and enforce them consistently with all employees.
   - Take all threats and inappropriate behavior seriously.
2. Have a multidisciplinary violence response team review every risk situation and choose the correct course of action, with the company prepared to do the following:

- Provide appropriate responses to stop outrageous behavior before it escalates.
- Do something sooner rather than later (after considering the legal issues).
- Conduct fitness-for-duty evaluations to see if the employee can continue to be on site.
- Use an employee assistance program or other psychotherapy and support services with the goal of restabilizing the employee.
- Have special referral sources and/or resources to deal with tough situations.
- Protect potential victims.
- Use security to protect the premises.
- Assess the risk potential of every termination and disciplinary action.
- Realize that discharged or disabled employees may still present a risk and follow them through the de-escalation process.

3. Train supervisors and managers at all levels of the organization, including the top layer, in skills needed for:
   - Conducting effective performance reviews
   - Conducting effective confrontations and making referrals for help
   - Developing an empowering management style, including interpersonal skills
   - Managing and leading without humiliating subordinates
   - Acquainting employees with employee assistance or other human resources people in non-problem-oriented roles so that they feel more comfortable seeking help when there is a problem

Senior management must set the tone and establish an expectation that these attitudes and actions will be carried out. By their words and behavior, top managers shape how other managers and supervisors react to employee behavior. It is the responsibility of top leadership to model the company's desire to make reactions nonpunitive and free of counterthreats or other escalation and to set an expectation that all threats will be investigated and immediate action taken when needed. Finally, senior management must plan ahead, not only to create the right kind of corporate culture, but also to have adequate security and other appropriate support resources available when they are needed.

In one semiconductor company, the company president makes it clear that there is no tolerance for violence. The first time somebody shoves or pushes someone else, the perpetrator is suspended. There are no inconsistencies in policy or decision making when it comes to the safety and well-being of all employees. Part of keeping the environment safe includes considering issues such as poor ventilation, excessive noise, unrealistic work pressures, and tedious tasks, all of which should be monitored in terms of the stress they create for employees.

Be Proactive in Managing Change

One way of viewing workplace violence is to think of the violence that is generally spreading through the country as spilling from the streets into the workplace. Perhaps a more worrisome perspective, and one that many people hold to, is that there is a growing level of employee rage being directed at the workplace. This rage is emerging increasingly in the form of workplace violence, as employees aim their work-related frustrations and desperation at victims who are seen as representatives of a company that the employee believes to be the source of his distress. This perspective on the growth of workplace violence considers the economic, social, and psychological factors that are now affecting the workforce at all levels of position through all types of industries. People who believe in this theory point to the "avenger phenomenon," a belief that the perpetrator of violence is trying to re-establish self-esteem or reduce overwhelming distress by getting even or retaliating for perceived harm or danger from the company or its representatives.

If you believe that the growth in workplace violence is partly an outgrowth of changes in the basic structure of employment, it is easy to identify four factors that may contribute to an increase in the "avenger phenomenon":

1. A poor economy and increased global competition that trigger layoffs and create employee resentment because

employers can no longer take care of their employees unconditionally, both in good times and bad times
2. A significant rise in the stress level in society generally, both on the job and off
3. A trend in our society increasingly to define people by their jobs, often resulting in a loss of self-worth when a person loses his job and has difficulty replacing it
4. The easy availability of guns and other types of weapons

Whatever the causes, it is clear that the changing workplace is contributing to the stress that employees and their bosses are experiencing. Forty-four percent of workers in the Northwestern National Life survey cited in Chapter 1 said their companies had cut jobs in the past year. Even the language used to describe what companies are doing with employees is violent. The words that are used are "take them out," "shoot them," "terminate them." The words reflect people's internal experience of what is going on. They are primitive and violent. Even relatively stable people can become unglued and violent in these highly stressful situations.

There are also certain organizational dynamics that can lead to the "avenger phenomenon" and that certainly allow and even encourage violence to occur. The Northwestern National Life Insurance Institute for Occupational Safety and Health survey of six hundred workers found that one in four had been attacked, threatened, or harassed on the job in the past year. One in six of those attacks involved a lethal weapon. These attacks occur partly because poorly trained supervisors trigger or reinforce intimidating behavior. Such supervisors fit in the authoritarian company cultures that deprive employees of dignity and respect and that stifle positive responses to threats. In my view, this underlying low-grade violence resulting from authoritative supervisory practices always reflects a failure by senior managers to develop the kind of corporate culture that is safe, honest, open, innovative, and productive. Given the level of ongoing job insecurity and the unsafe environments in which many people work, it is easy to see how employees may increasingly view their companies as indifferent or even malevolent forces.

As part of a preventive strategy, employers need to learn to terminate employees in an effective manner. Senior management must make the practical business decision to do this because the costs of doing otherwise outweigh the costs of doing it correctly. Since job loss can trigger violence, companies planning reductions must be sensitive to the needs of the employees affected. This sensitivity must take the form of giving as much advanced notice as possible, handling layoffs fairly, and providing reasonable severance benefits, if at all possible. The rationale for the layoffs must be stated clearly and repeatedly in a credible manner. Employees need to be overinformed rather than kept in the dark about what is happening and why. It is only within this context that the staff handling the layoffs can learn to avoid arguments over the merits of the decision, to focus on the person's future in a positive way, to listen to the employee's reactions both in words and in body language, to help the person recover from the blow to his self-esteem and optimism, and to set a tone that is controlled, positive, and focused.

Chapter 9

Downsizing and Terminations

In every business, downsizing, or the planned elimination of jobs, raises fears that laid-off workers will respond with violence. Downsizing has become pervasive in the corporate world of the 1990s. Hardly a day goes by that we do not read of several companies eliminating significant percentages of their workforces. Even though we think that most workplace violence is perpetuated by a single employee who is being terminated for cause, large-scale terminations can evoke the same personalized and negative feelings of stress and rejection as individual termination situations. Therefore, it is important for employers to carefully consider how they conduct mass layoffs and plant closings.

Effective Downsizing: Difficult but Possible

Since 1987, about 85 percent of the thousand largest U.S. companies have reduced their workforces through downsizing. Wayne Cascio, in the *Academy of Management Executive*, reviewed more than five hundred research studies on downsizing and found that in about half of the companies, neither the economic nor the organizational benefits that were anticipated were in fact realized. Until there is a change in the conditions that cause companies to downsize, workforce reductions are likely to continue. For the present, overhead in U.S. companies is still significantly higher than it is for companies in other countries, and U.S. companies continue to carry much higher levels of debt payments than in the past.

A 1994 American Management Association survey found that one fourth of companies planned to cut payroll during the next year, the highest rate in six years. Year-end audits show that the number of companies that actually make reductions is double the number that plan or announce reductions, suggesting that many company downsizings are not planned very far in advance. It may be this lack of preparation that leads to such poor results from most downsizing.

Many research studies indicate that downsizing does not produce the expected cost savings. In fact, there are many negative consequences from downsizing, and profitability does not necessarily improve. Of more than five hundred companies that reduced their workforces over a six-year period, as studied by Cascio, only 43.5 percent subsequently increased their operating profits. Nor did productivity increase in the majority of companies. In most of the 1,468 companies surveyed that had "restructured," productivity either stayed the same or deteriorated after layoffs.

More than 50 percent of companies that downsize find that their expense levels creep back up. A study of 1,005 companies found that one out of five companies replaced some of the positions that had been eliminated. In addition, downsizing can have many other negative effects. Continuous downsizing has left middle managers less optimistic about their chances for advancement. Unlike previous economic downturns, the recession of the early 1990s led to a significant reduction in the number of white-collar workers, who, in 1994, constituted 36 percent of the unemployed, compared to 22 percent in the last recession. Middle-level managers have been especially hard hit. While they constitute 5 to 8 percent of the average workforce, they represent 17 percent of all dismissals from 1989 to 1991 and 19 percent of dismissals in 1992. The study found that while 75 percent of managers felt positive about their careers in 1979, fewer than a third felt optimistic in 1992. Other surveys indicate that there is less employee loyalty to companies today than in earlier decades. The average company tenure of departing managers has dropped by an average of five years compared to average tenure in 1981. Other studies show that workers under age 35 stay on a job a median of only 2.5 years.

Many studies have shown that downsizing results in the surviving employees' becoming narrowly focused, risk-averse, and self-absorbed. The vast majority of companies that have downsized report afterward that their workers have low morale, are fearful of losing their jobs, and distrust management. Clearly, the majority of companies that downsize do not get the results they are expecting.

So what do the one third of companies that get the results they are seeking from downsizing do right? A study by K. S. Cameron found six general strategies that enable companies to improve organizational effectiveness while downsizing:

1. Company leaders initiated the downsizing, and they remained visible and involved throughout the process.

2. Management left the actual downsizing design to employees who analyzed the operations of the organization job by job and task by task. Rather than just reducing numbers, the employees set priorities on where to downsize, while redesigning the organization with a goal of systemic, long-term change for those remaining within the company.

3. Effective companies paid particular attention to those who were not cut, recognizing that they typically experienced emotional reactions in addition to having to take on more work.

4. Successful companies made special efforts to communicate a positive message, open up two-way communication, and increase the level of training with remaining employees. In short, the downsizing effort was not focused just on eliminating positions but rather on evaluating the company's entire system of suppliers, customers, and distributors, improving all aspects of its operations.

5. Successful companies learned to tailor the smaller organization to new market and internal needs rather than simply decentralizing. They created small, semiautonomous organizations in operating units and large, integrated organizations to eliminate duplication and reduce costs. The key to the simultaneous use of small and large organizations during downsizing was a "clan" type of control system that relies on common values,

shared vision, and a collective perspective, rather than on a traditional control system.

6. The most successful organizations targeted lower head count as a central, critical outcome but also presented downsizing to their employees as just one in a cluster of strategies designed to achieve organizational improvement.

The best way to accomplish downsizing in order to leave remaining employees with higher morale and better productivity parallels the best way to prevent violence from those who are forced out of the company. In the painful change process created by downsizing, companies can take a number of actions to manage the reactions of those affected, whether they are staying or leaving:

1. There must be a clear message about why the change is being made so that workers do not personalize their own experience. The message should include a credible and clear rationale for the action, consistently repeated over and over again until employees understand and believe it.

2. Top management needs to lead the change effort. It cannot afford to isolate itself and leave the work to others.

Employee relations or human resources personnel should not be turned into scapegoats. Since tough decisions will continue to be required in the rapidly changing and highly competitive marketplace of the 1990s, senior managers must personally take responsibility for communicating in a believable and informative manner the rationales for these decisions. They must also present the business context that necessitates the changes and explain how the actions will improve the company's odds of succeeding in its marketplace.

When special job actions are taken, such as downsizing, significant job reassignment, or threats of closing units or divisions, it is likely that every employee's sense of identity and security will be threatened. This is especially true when the employee's central sense of identity comes from his work. The level of stress aroused can provoke violent reactions. Three critical factors, however, can mitigate against a violent reaction:

1. How the employees are given the message
2. What they believe were the real reasons behind the decisions
3. How fair they believe the selection process to be by which employees were chosen for termination

Lower-level employees are not the only ones who have difficulty dealing with major transitions in the workforce. Managers can also react in bizarre and irrational ways. Even those responsible for the decisions can exhibit highly inappropriate, purely emotional behaviors. Have you heard the story about the managers who wore bulletproof vests while they handed out pink slips? It's a true story. Imagine the impact this action must have had on everyone. One executive's plan for handling a downsizing was to tell each worker he was fired and then escort him immediately out the door, never to return again. There was not a thought to using available internal resources or hiring external ones, such as counseling or outplacement services to provide support for the exiting employees. There was no recognition that an employee, suddenly abandoned and humiliated, might become so enraged and hurt that he might return with a weapon to get even. It was not that this executive was an insensitive person. The fact was just the opposite. He was having so much trouble dealing with his own feelings about what he was doing to the employees, about whom he cared very much, that he was simply trying to put the whole thing out of his mind.

Announcing the Bad News

Planning the Announcement

How a company prepares, tells, and handles its employees in the separation and layoff process is critical in reducing the possibility of violence. Proper planning is the starting point in doing any downsizing well. One important part of such planning is deciding which potentially available resources, such as outplacement and employee assistance programs, psychological counseling, severance benefits, retraining and skills development, and educational assistance, will be used. The tradeoffs between the costs of providing support services for terminating employees and the costs of defending potential legal actions by litigious, unhappy former employees should be weighed.

Decisions should made about which services will be offered before any news is announced. Support services can be critical in reducing the risk of violent reactions during employee separations at all levels of the organization, from the shop floor to the executive suite. They provide a source for monitoring employees' responses, de-escalate rising tensions and stress, and build coping strategies that enhance self-esteem and options for a person who might otherwise become overwhelmed and desperate.

The timing of notification and action also needs to be planned. Senior managers tend to share a common reaction, which is to get the whole thing over with as quickly as possible once the decision has been made. They are concerned about the discomfort that people may feel knowing that they or a co-worker will be leaving under difficult circumstances. But the "tell them and walk them out the door" philosophy leaves no room for grieving and for saying good-byes. People need time to adjust to the news and to let go of each other emotionally. Often, they also need time to shift their responsibilities to someone else. I am not saying that employees should be required to stay on the job and pretend that nothing has changed after they've received their notice. I am suggesting that management, out of fear and discomfort, sometimes throws terminated employees summarily off the grounds in a way that leaves the employees with a sense of isolation and desertion. These feelings can elicit violent reactions and deprive them of the opportunity to do an adequate job of emotionally letting go.

One of the most common mistakes in planning downsizing is to think that human resources or outplacement services can accomplish the task alone. While their support, guidance, and coordination can be very useful in planning and successfully accomplishing staff reductions, the remaining managers have a critical role to play in the process, from announcing the news to dealing with the aftermath. While some companies turn downsizing processes over to their human resources professionals, there are some tremendous benefits from involving current supervisors and managers in the process, including helping them work through their own emotions of letting go and preparing them to deal with the survivors for whom they still have responsibility. It also allows them proactively to deal with the intense reactions that all the employees will have. The only way that they can do this is by continually communicating with employees in a supportive and monitoring way. They need to simultaneously accomplish three tasks:

1. Coordinate and assist in the smooth transition of job responsibilities from those who are leaving to those who are taking on their jobs.
2. Monitor the reactions of those who are leaving and assist them in responding constructively from the point that they first hear the news until the transition process is completed.
3. Communicate a sincere and genuine interest in the employees' well-being.

A critical issue in successful downsizing is training management to demonstrate caring and appropriate interest in the future welfare of the individuals who are leaving, whatever the reasons. Many people recommend developing a termination script to be used both by the person who must stand up in front of everyone to make the formal announcements and by the individual managers who must break the news to individual employees. It is not uncommon for senior management and the company's legal department to write a script for themselves and others to follow closely. The danger of sounding mechanical and without humanity is overwhelming in employing this tactic, and I don't recommend it. More useful training for managers includes teaching helping skills, such as listening, giving feedback, and responding to feelings. The focus should be on how to be real and congruent (how to make sure their words, feelings, and body language match).

However, it is important that management ensure that everyone involved in handling the downsizing has an accurate and thoughtful rationale for the termination and is able to spell it out clearly. Managers should be prepared to explain the business reasons for the reductions and to list the factors contributing to the need for the reduction. They should be prepared also to explain how all decisions were made and reviewed. In addition to being able to explain the rationale and process used in the downsizing, managers must be ready to deal with employees' logistical questions. All severance information should be prepared in writing, including a notification letter that delineates working and nonworking notice, salary continuation, severance period, benefits, outplacement counseling, and other pertinent information. The information should include the date that the separation is effective and salary continuation and benefits. If it does not, management should arrange for an employee relations representative to provide this information as soon as possible. Managers need to be sufficiently familiar with the outplacement assistance or other safety nets that have been arranged to be able to describe and answer questions about them. It is important to state clearly that the company has paid for the services.

In situations where the employee is to be removed from the site immediately for security purposes, the manager needs to understand how and when the person may collect her personal belongings. If the safety of the person, of co-workers, of equipment, or of information is at risk, it may be appropriate to arrange to have an escort for the employee. This idea should be introduced only after the employee has had time to regain his composure after hearing the news. In planning for appropriate escorts, you might consider the company's security officer or selected managers or co-workers who are seen as friendly or supportive.

Offering Supportive Services

Extended outplacement services and other assistance are typically provided away from the worksite so that terminated employees can maintain some sense of privacy. This arrangement also allows them to separate the provider of the services from the company. For many employees experiencing downsizing, this system allows them to use the services to work through their anger and other feelings about the company.

Many outplacement firms recommend that outplacement

services be provided on site immediately after the meeting at which the individual employee is told he is going to be terminated. This can help deflect the individual's anger from the company by getting him to start focusing right away on future career plans and to help him see that assistance will be available. The outplacement counselor needs to know all the reasons for the terminations. The facts need to be clear and consistently understood by everyone involved in the process.

Breaking the News

Before the manager conducts the termination meeting, she should make sure that nothing is known to indicate that the employee has a history of violent or intimidating behavior that should be investigated. For employees with a history of any violent behavior, an employee assistance counselor can be brought on site to provide immediate follow-up counseling for the individual after the termination meeting.

Managers need to be trained on how to handle properly the notification process and how to respond appropriately to different reactions. A critical part of this preparation is for the manager to anticipate and be prepared to deal with her own emotional reactions to breaking the news. Managers must realize that the downsizing is neither their fault nor the employee's; nor is it the executive's. Besides guilt, the major emotional response managers are most likely to have is pain, which can feel overwhelming. Severe pain can lead to avoidance. No matter what else managers do, if they avoid their own emotional reactions to the situation, they will come across as so cold and uncaring as to be provocative. Managers should be sure to allow time to plan, organize, and practice the steps for termination, keeping their own emotional reactions in mind. It is through solid preparation and practice that they will improve their ability to handle their emotions as they give what may seem like the worst news the person has ever received.

If the termination process is done well, former employees will feel that their self-esteem has been protected and that they have been treated with dignity. Equally important, they will leave the organization feeling as positive as possible.

If you are a manager who has the challenge of actually breaking the news, you must first, set the tone for the meeting and maintain focus. You need to provide the facts in a way that the employee can understand and grasp. To accomplish that goal, you need to show concern while remaining professional. You need to be clear about the rationale by which individuals were selected and be able to explain it in a simple, direct manner. It is important that you not avoid giving the employee the message, but at the same time you do not want to hit her over the head with the news, either. One way to monitor your effectiveness is to be aware of the employee's body language. If she is making eye contact, you know she is listening. Another way to monitor how the employee is receiving your message is to listen to what the employee has to say.

Don't do all the talking. Include pauses and speak at a moderate pace so that the employee has an opportunity to verbalize her reactions as she feels the need. Don't overload her with information. You want to get across the basic message that she has been selected; that is all that matters in this initial conversation. Don't argue over the correctness of the decision. Make sure the employee understands the message. If necessary, repeat or restate the information. Listen actively and ask questions to confirm that the employee understands your message. You can even ask the employee to restate the information if you think she is not understanding what you are saying. Your goal in this initial meeting is not to help the employee work through her emotions but only to break the news and provide the facts about the next steps, including becoming ready to hear about the benefits and services that the company will be making available. Emotionally, you want to help the employee begin to realize that the message is real. It can be helpful to ask the employee if she understands the message and to repeat it.

Even in situations where everyone knows what is coming, there is always a degree of shock or denial when the employee actually hears the words spoken. It can have tremendous emotional impact to hear that you have lost your job or that your career at the company is over. The manager should expect disbelief or shock during this initial meeting. Since part of the manager's goal is to help the employee move through the termination process, you need to deal with this emotional reaction in the employee. You do this in part by providing opportunities for the employee to express her emotions. Simply listen and acknowledge them. Such effusion is part of the process of moving beyond the initial reaction. By being sympathetic and understanding throughout, the manager can break the news while helping the employee maintain his sense of self-esteem. It is important to keep the entire meeting as positive as possible in tone and to focus on the positive aspects of the terminated person's future, using the services the company will provide as part of a strategy for moving on. The final part of the meeting should include an offer to set up a follow-up appointment with the employee and to arrange an appointment with the support services being offered, rather than leaving this for the employee to do on his own.

In order to deliver such difficult news effectively to an employee, you must first have dealt with your own pain and anxiety about the situation. The best way to do this is to talk out your feelings with others so that you are clear about what you are feeling and thinking about the entire situation and about the individual employee. Only when you reach some degree of genuine comfort or at least honesty with yourself can you be ready to break the news.

Sometimes when you deliver the news, the terminated employee will become quite angry. You must prepare for this possibility in two ways. One is by doing your homework so that you know if the employee has a history of any violent or intimidating behavior. The other is to prepare yourself for the possibility that the employee will react with blame and anger and to have rehearsed your responses and anticipated how you will feel.

Having done your homework, you should be able to do the right things, including staying calm and not becoming defensive. Remember, you do not have to or even want to try to change the employee's attitude or response during this initial meeting. You do not want to escalate the tension he may already be feeling. You certainly do not want to argue about anything. Let the employee express how he is feeling. Such venting may release pressure by itself.

Don't feel you have to control or influence the employee's

reaction. Simply acknowledge what you hear as the person's feelings and try to understand his perspective. This conversation can provide you with important information that may be critical later on in assessing the person's risk of becoming violent. It can also help you later if you need to develop strategies for de-escalating a potential or actual crisis with the person. Of course, your responses during the conversation will be directed in part to trying to defuse the tension that the person is feeling. Sometimes humor or lightness can help in this process, but you must be very careful to not appear flip or demeaning. If you have prepared in advance to face the person's anger, you will be better able to focus your comments during the meeting and to remain as neutral and nonprovocative as possible. You should also have important phone numbers for or other ways of contacting key resources such as security, human resources, employee relations, employee assistance, or occupational health and medical services, if their assistance should be necessary.

Regardless of how the interview goes, it is typically not very long or involved. Toward the end, you will want to review with the employee a little about the benefits and services that will be available to assist her. By addressing the next steps in the process, you ensure that the employee is not left with a sense of hanging out there on her own, and you and the company do not appear rejecting or uncaring. This can help to defuse the employee's anger or denial. In fact, it can help the individual focus on the task at hand, rather than getting lost in emotionality.

Often the next step, taken immediately or shortly after the termination meeting, is a meeting with an outplacement or employee assistance counselor. If the counselor is perceived as a neutral party or as an advocate for the employee rather than an agent of the company, the employee can begin to discuss her reactions to the news. As trust and comfort develop, the employee will become more willing and able to hear about the available help.

Anticipating the Reaction

People who become violent during the termination process usually do so later rather than earlier in the process. They think about and emotionally react to what has happened. These reactions build over time until they spill into violent behavior. In accordance with the basic model I have described of how behavior spirals into violence, the company needs to manage both the cognitive and the emotional aspects of this process.

On the emotional side, the employee must go successfully through some predictable stages of reaction. This process is perhaps best described by the stages through which a person passes in reaction to finding out that she is dying. These stages were described by Dr. Elizabeth Kübler-Ross in her classic book, *On Death and Dying*. The most common initial reaction is denial or shock, accompanied by self-isolating behavior. The passage of time, the assertion of reality, and support from others help the person through this stage. Just because a person has been told "you're fired" does not mean that she really believes it. It is part of the role of outplacement to help employees know that there is life beyond the company and that accepting reality does not have to shatter the other aspects of their lives. It is amazing how many employees cannot tell their spouses of their job losses, because they cannot deal with the loss of self-esteem that accompanies admitting the reality to themselves or the fear that the spouses will think them failures.

As denial falls away, it is replaced by bargaining and anger. The employee may want to argue about the merits of the decision in order to find a way to reverse the decision. The louder the employee or executive talks, the softer the manager should talk. It is very important to avoid confrontation because the employee cannot have a one-sided argument. The manager will not win a discussion about whether the company is making the right decision; he can only provoke the employee more. Anger is a natural part of reacting to a significant loss.

The other side of anger is depression, and the combination can lead the employee to want to blame someone. Sometimes the person's depression and anger can become desperation, particularly if she sees the job loss as an insurmountable catastrophe. Such a way of thinking leads to a feeling of hopelessness. A person reacting in this way should immediately be referred to an employee assistance or other professional counselor.

The last stage in Kübler-Ross's schema is depression. It is

normal for employees to feel depressed in response to the impending loss of friends, of the familiar, of status, of security, and
of their sense of themselves and their world. Only if they become
hopeless or fail to take the actions necessary to move on with
their lives is depression worrisome.

Only after going through a period of substantial emotional
turmoil does the person come to accept the reality of what is
happening to him. The pain is gone from the surface. Resignation
has taken over. Then life can go forward.

Some employees may react to news of their termination with
fear, loss, guilt, betrayal, suspicion, mistrust, outrage, or detach-
ment. At each stage of dealing with job loss, the manager needs
to look for signs that the person is coping with whatever stage
she is in.

In response to the crisis of job loss, people can either take
on the role of victim or rally to new opportunities and possibilities. If the person responds with reality-oriented questions about
next steps, follow-up, severance arrangements, and timing, it is
likely that he is getting over the bad news and focusing on the
future. On the other hand, if the person is stuck in the early stages
of denial or depression, desperate actions may be the result. By
continuing to monitor the employee's state of mind, the manager
can provide useful support and serve as an early warning system
if the stress of the termination begins to overwhelm the employee's ability to cope.

Like most downsizing, most corporate mergers fail to attain
their expected goals. Eighty percent of mergers eventually fall
short, perhaps because they don't handle the emotional needs
of employees well. This is reflected in the difficulties most senior
management groups have in integrating employees from different companies after a merger. There is every reason to believe
that this difficulty affects the entire organization.

While some senior managers, human resources vice presidents among them, still say that the human issues aren't important, the facts point to the need for employees to verbalize their
concerns and to be listened to at all levels of the company. When
major job shifts are occurring within a company, it is critical that
the senior executive meet with workers and tell them what's
really going on. If the president or chief executive officer doesn't

face the employees directly, head to head and heart to heart, it looks as if the company has something to hide or dramatic changes in employees' status don't matter because employees don't matter. It probably takes real courage for an executive to stand up in front of a group of employees facing the possible or actual loss of their jobs and to let employees ask him the hard questions. But unless labor and management representatives and staff at all levels throughout the company are put in the same room to talk honestly about their perceptions and feelings, how can they work together? There is a natural division between the decision makers and those affected by the downsizing process, and it is easy for animosities to develop. In such a context, it is very easy for individuals to take offense, to personalize pressures, and to feel singled out.

It is the role of senior management to see that these chasms are bridged. One way to accomplish this reintegration is to use impartial third parties to bring people together. The goal of such meetings is to let the remaining employees ventilate and to help them understand the company's new direction and approach, which provides the context for the downsizing. These meetings should result in team building for those who remain in the organization. During such discussions, it is important to identify employees who need individual assistance. Those who seem locked rigidly into an anticompany stance and are loners could become dangerous, because they are not open to going beyond the blame and suspicion that mark the initial stages of downsizing, mergers, and major organizational redesigns. If the factors used in selecting the survivors are not identified, reviewed, and uniformly applied, or if the criteria are not communicated in a credible and clear manner to the workforce, it becomes easy for individual employees to see favoritism, bias, and worse. Those perceptions can lead to violence.

Beneath the anger, most people are frightened and confused by the multitude of changes going on in the workplace. These feelings can exacerbate the natural dichotomy between decision makers and those affected by their decisions. To counter this tendency, senior managers must make themselves visible and open to dialogue. Employees who feel vulnerable must have someone to talk to if they feel the need. If management can identify those employees who have gotten caught in the denial or anger stages of downsizing and get them help, they will have gone a very long way in protecting the company from workplace violence.

Going On: Dealing With the Survivors

From a purely business point of view, corporate leaders must be concerned that the odds are that downsizing will not achieve the cost savings that it is designed to accomplish. If a major reason for this failure has to do with the human reactions to the process, then senior managers must be concerned with the psychological issues, as well. They have to be aware that those who remain in the company following major downsizing may suffer symptoms of trauma that will both interfere with their effectiveness and lower productivity. These reactions are commonly part of the aftermath of the severe emotional stress and strain that employees experience as they go through the loss of co-workers and face uncertainty about their own futures. The chief cure for trauma, as described in Chapter 7, is to let employees talk about their experience. By acknowledging their reactions and feelings, managers can help them come to grips with what has happened to them and help them move past it.

For both psychological and business reasons, it seems clear that senior managers need to consider how and what to tell the employees who remain. Here's how to plan and communicate in a timely way around the issues of downsizing.

1. Let your employees know ahead of time what is going to happen: the rationale, the timing, and the process by which fair and wise decision making will occur. Do not surprise them and do not leave them in the dark to generate any more rumors than you have to, since the rumors will be rampant and grossly incorrect anyway. To the degree that business conditions allow, it is better to do damage control up-front, giving employees as many facts as you can accurately and reliably present.

2. Communicate both in writing and in person. Meet face

to face with your employees, in small groups, large audiences, or even teleconferences. Leave time for questions and answers and sharing of reactions from all sides of the decision making. It is not sufficient to simply send out a memo.

3. On the day you announce the terminations, or soon thereafter, meet with your employees to review the day's events. Restate the business reasons for the terminations that are given in the written explanation. Place the layoffs in the wider environmental and strategic context of the business, such as changes in regulations, competition, industrial segments, market conditions, or technology. If you have rethought your division or corporate goals and strategies to align with strategies for future success, present this thinking. Presumably this was the basis on which management decided where and how to make reductions in staffing. If these goals and strategies are made clear, the remaining employees will be able to understand where the company is heading and how to direct their own efforts. It is this understanding that will help them determine what changes must be made in managing their own workloads. They will be able to foresee the necessary work transitions and plan how to make them easier for those who are leaving and for those who are staying.

4. As a manager, become visible and accessible to your own department during the process. Proactively answer questions, provide direction, and curtail rumors. By giving all employees the chance to talk about their personal career concerns and reactions to the company's changes, managers provide structure, support, and focus on short-term goals that help employees cope with the changes and reorient themselves to the altered worksite.

5. Reach out to higher performers. This is of particular importance, as this is the group at greatest risk of leaving the organization during the chaos of change. By involving them in the changes and recognizing their importance, managers can help them become positive influences on other, more vulnerable employees.

6. Managers must prepare their employees for the prolonged recovery period that is likely after any significant workforce changes. Much has been written of survivor guilt. Whatever

one thinks of that concept, it is clear that downsizing has significant impact on those who remain. The process is not over when the exiting employees have left. Various work groups transition at different rates. Managers and executives need to be prepared to respond to the aftereffects of the downsizing for a long time after the event.

Inherent in these recommendations about how to deal with the survivors are some basic assumptions. You shouldn't try to control the uncontrollable. Overcontrol can result in pushing feelings and thoughts underground, where they can mushroom into reactions that cannot be processed within the organization. The processes that prevent this from happening are characterized by open and honest two-way communication. They show respect for and trust in the people being affected by the changes. They acknowledge differences in perspective and the range of feelings people may be having. Most of all, they focus on the basic business goals and strategy that provided the basis for the changes. With this kind of communication, company leaders can help employees develop a sense of their own control and empowerment, even during times of downsizing. Because information is power, this dialogue helps to create adult-to-adult relationships in a situation where some employees could easily feel treated like children and react accordingly. It sets the tone for negotiating win-win discussions, even with those who are leaving the company.

Executives should never have the illusion that those remaining in the workforce are not looking at how the employees who are leaving are being treated. The way downsizing occurs becomes a powerful message to those who remain about how the company sees its employees and what employees can expect from the company in the future. Managers should never underestimate the importance of the messages they send by how they are dealing with exiting employees. If the process has been fair, if people have been treated with respect, if senior managers have been open with their feelings and perspectives and have given clear and credible rationales for their decisions, then employees can share their own reactions honestly and reach new levels of empowerment and participation in the new organization. Old tensions can be overcome and new work partnerships forged. On the other hand, if the downsizing is not done effectively, individuals may descend into a morass of depression, denial, blame, job insecurity, resentment, and confusion to the point of becoming violent. A frequent sign that downsizing has failed is a promise by senior executives that it will never happen again. Such false promises compromise credibility and generate a culture of mistrust and suspicion. Never say "Never again."

Denial of emotions is often the most pervasive reaction to downsizing among senior managers. The fact is that executives are people, too, and they often feel great pressure to keep stock prices and morale up. They may attempt to do so by not sharing their own feelings and instead giving only positive messages in an attempt to convince observers that "everything will work out." They tend to isolate themselves and to undercommunicate during difficult and sensitive periods, such as during downsizing. Many executives are not psychologically astute or intuitive about what their employees need from them. Because they feel responsible for the pain they are inflicting, many feel an enormous tendency to avoid the "victims" and thus end up creating a sense of even more severe rejection in those being terminated.

Many senior executives feel overwhelmed and emotionally drained by their own reactions to the decisions they have made. Employees in their organizations are eager to be heard by those at the top. There is a need to reestablish some sense of control by both the survivors and those leaving. This can be done through interactive dialogue with the decision makers. Executives need to make themselves approachable, real, and engaging. They need to appreciate that they cannot provide the whole resolution to the feelings and problems created by downsizing. They should not even try. Instead, they must realize that sharing their humanity with their employees helps build trust and teamwork and gives others permission to be honest and participatory. Such behavior can help establish ways for employees to care for each other in the adult ways that fit in the new social employment contract of employer and employee.

A Company That Did It Right: Best Practices

For downsizing to produce the desired effects in a company's bottom line and for it to be effective in preventing violence, it is critical that a clear and believable business rationale explaining the need for the change be communicated to all employees; that the rationale fit into a larger competitive strategy for the company so that employees know how to direct their own efforts constructively; that the process of selecting who is kept be done in a way that is perceived as fair and equitable; and that the process used to accomplish the task respect the dignity and worth of all involved. Survivors see how the company treats those who are leaving, and this greatly affects their beliefs about the leaders of the company and about what they can expect from them in the future. These beliefs in turn considerably impact survivors' performance in the new organization and their potential to become violent.

I had the opportunity to assist the packaged-goods division of a large company through a downsizing that went well and that was handled in a way that represents a radical departure from the typical process. As a result, the company had little litigation and no violent threats or events. I believe other companies can learn from its good example.

The division was profitable but faced increasingly intense pressures from competitors in its marketplace. Its customers were rapidly consolidating and demanding lower profit margins and a different level of value-added service from what the division was experienced in providing. As the result of two acquisitions in the 1980s, the division consisted of three distinct groups. Each group had its own name brands and corporate culture. Many functions among the three were duplicative, creating costly redundancies internally and complications and confusion for customers externally. The situation was a typical precursor of a downsizing effort. In this case, however, rather than just seeking to reduce costs by eliminating a certain number of positions, the leadership had the vision to look at the larger strategic goals of the division. What it saw was a need to reduce costs, become more flexible and responsive to ongoing changes in the marketplace, and simplify and improve the company's way of working with customers.

The division's first step was to plan what it needed to do. The decision was made to trim the workforce by $5 million to $8 million immediately, while looking for additional savings that could be gained through attrition and more gradual reductions over time. Rather than stop there, however, the division's leadership realized that it needed to develop and communicate a new vision of what the company needed to provide in the marketplace to position itself for future success with its customers.

Out of its strategy discussions, the leadership team made a second critical decision. Rather than going behind closed doors to decide which employees were staying and which were leaving, it decided to create a process that would evaluate the abilities of all current employees in order to determine which workers could best help drive the division toward its goals. In the past, the company would have looked at past performance and rewarded the best performers by retaining them. The problem with that method of selecting whom to keep was that the new organization needed to do business in a significantly different way from in the past and therefore needed to choose individuals who had the skill sets needed for the future. Nor would the traditional closed-room selection process adequately communicate to the remaining employees that it was not going to be business as usual.

For these reasons, the leadership set two goals: to choose the best candidates for the future needs of the company from the current employee pool and, at the same time, to help those who remained in the company understand that what would be expected of them in the future would be significantly different from their current way of working. The leadership team also believed that how it dealt with its workforce through this process had to be consistent with the division's values statement. The division's written values statement already articulated all of the key practices that help a company create an effective work environment and prevent violence, such as respecting all employees, treating them honestly and fairly, and empowering them with the knowledge necessary for them to develop a sense of ownership for the success or failure of the business.

To accomplish their goals while putting their values into practice, the company chose a process of selecting the survivors that initially created great uncertainty both in the workforce and in the company's customers. Since the sales division was the interface with the customer, every job in that part of the organization was reevaluated. Using an outside firm that specializes in redesign, employees and customers were solicited for ideas on how to organize the sales force more effectively and how to define the critical tasks to surpass future competition. This information was used to redesign the organization and all of the important jobs needed within it for the future. On the basis of this thinking, the division delineated the critical success factors for each new position in the downsized organization. Success factors included skill sets, interpersonal abilities, relevant personality traits, and customer perceptions. The factors cut across the behavioral styles of the division's three existing cultures and defined what was central to the new culture the organization was striving to create.

An interdisciplinary team from across the division was trained to interview using the success factors defined for each position. Current employees were allowed to apply for any position they chose. If they met the basic qualifications listed in the job description, they were interviewed and rated on an objective scale by each member of the interview team. Initially, many employees questioned why they had to interview for what they considered to be "their" jobs. As they went through the selection process, they discovered the wisdom of the process. They had to read each job description carefully to determine how the contents differed from what they were currently doing or what they thought would be expected in the position in the future. If the company was not simply going to use the "old boy" school of selection, based on who knows whom, what would top management be looking for? Many employees began to put together thoughts about what was going to be important to the division for its future success. They got the message that it was not business as usual.

As they went through their interviews, employees also began to understand that the process was not just a sham to make them feel fairly considered. They were actually being reevaluated and given a chance to present themselves. They were asked incisive questions about the future of the business. They were treated like potential shareholders. Their responses were listened to carefully and investigated further. In addition, finalists were put through a psychological assessment to see if their motivations, personalities, intellects, and interpersonal styles fit with the desired culture of the downsized organization. All of the information was then debriefed by the interview group. Members challenged one another's perceptions of how a particular individual would perform and shared their own views of where the company was going. After the top level of the organization was selected, those who were chosen joined the interview team and selected the next layer, all the way down the organization.

At first glance, this process may appear elaborate, expensive, or time-consuming. In fact, it was finished in five months and accomplished all of the critical goals that the division's leaders had established to reposition the company for the future.

1. The process reduced costs by about $3 million the first year, with up to double that number in savings for every year thereafter.

2. It resulted in the choice of the best people from the existing employee pool, those who could meet the future needs of the company as it competed in its changing marketplace.

3. It clearly communicated to the employees who remained that things were not business as usual. It even helped them understand what others in leadership positions were expecting and made them think about both the directions they thought the company should be taking and their own skill sets for getting the company there.

4. The process itself modeled a quality of leader-employee relationship that set the tone for the future. It helped shape a new divisional culture in which people are treated with respect and consideration while being held accountable in a new way for the success of the business. Before the interview process, all employees were given summaries of the redesign study outlining the problems and issues in the current practice and the goals

and purposes of organizational redesign. The new structure was spelled out so that all employees could see the larger picture into which they might fit. The report and the conversations through which it was first developed and later clarified for employees gave the process a business improvement focus rather than a focus on simply lopping off a few positions.

5. The process put into practice the values articulated by the division leadership. It created a new level of openness about the competitive issues of the business and a new personal level of honesty about feedback and confrontation. Employees participating in the interview teams learned a great deal about each other. They found out how much people cared about the success of the company. They learned how empathic and caring their co-workers were. They shared individual ideas about the hard business issues the division faced. This new level of teamwork, honesty, and direct engagement with the reality of the market-place went a long way toward making the division what it had to be to succeed in its marketplace in the future.

The impact of the selection process on those who went through it was profound. Employees realized the reality of the changes in the workplace and discovered a new admiration for the company's leaders. Of course, there were those who did not receive offers to stay in the organization. After each round of interviewing and decision making, the new hiring manager for the position under consideration spoke with each employee/applicant to let him know if he was going to be offered the position. It was at this point that the considerable pain involved in downsizing became real to the participants. Part of the interview group debriefing meetings had dealt with anticipating the feelings of those who were not being selected and helping the decision makers in the group begin to deal with their own feelings. These sessions had been heart-wrenching and draining. But the emotional reality had not yet hit.

In the course of the interviewing and selection process, it became clear that nervous employees were talking to each other and to customers, more out of their fears than out of any informed reality. Rumors became rampant. Something had to be done to control the potential damage and to lower the anxiety level of employees, which was at the heart of the problem. Human resources personnel tried successfully to remain neutral so that later they could assist employees in using outplacement and severance services. After initial resistance, senior management was finally convinced that the division managers needed to take responsibility for managing the anxiety and perceptions of employees through the downsizing process. In essence, managers were given two new roles in addition to performing their normal jobs. They had to prepare to interview for the positions in the redesigned organization that they sought, and they had to manage their subordinates through the process. This was accomplished by having managers proactively reach out to their work groups to check on rumors, to answer questions, and to defuse tension with support and accurate information. The rationale for the downsizing and the justification of the process had to be restated repeatedly. Just as important, employees needed to feel someone was listening to them.

Because telling someone you have worked with for years that she is being moved out of the company is a very hard task, a reputable outplacement firm had been engaged at the beginning of the process and the managers had been informed about the services that would be available and how to access them. The human resources staff had also prepared clear and generous severance packages and explained to the managers the process of communicating severance information to employees who were not being retained. However, it was the hiring manager's responsibility to inform each employee/applicant whether she had been selected for the position she sought.

Where possible, termination conversations were held in person in a private room. If that was not possible, a supportive local manager was placed in the room next door to the employee so that after the phone call, there could be immediate face-to-face contact to monitor the individual's responses and coping ability. The managers were given guidelines about how to deliver the news, with emphasis on being caring, responsive, and in most cases brief. The message was: "You have many strengths and much to offer, but you are not seen as a better fit than someone else for where we are trying to go now as a company. We will help you move on." Follow-up steps were scripted, but not the

conversation itself. Managers also did some role playing to prepare themselves to deal with their own emotions and with the
reactions they expected to receive from the other person. Their
own feelings were acknowledged and discussed. It was painful
and moving for all concerned.

The managers did a good job of keeping the decisions confidential until the announcement date. Immediately after the news
was given to the workforce, the employee's manager, a human
resources professional, and the management psychologists who
were supporting the process discussed each employee's reaction.
An intervention was planned for each employee who appeared
to be having a particularly difficult reaction. This monitoring of
each employee continued in the days ahead. Some employees
were connected to the employee assistance program for support.
Most met with a counselor from the outplacement firm. Managers did not use the availability of other support services as an
excuse to avoid actively participating in the ongoing dialogue
with all employees. This communicated to those terminated that
the company was not deserting them, that they were not pariahs,
and that they had a future.

Some employees had a difficult time. Some became very
angry; some got quite depressed. Anyone who needed it received
help without having to ask for it. The need was obvious to those
who were monitoring workers' reactions. The result was that
there was neither violence nor any threat of violence. Those who
left the company departed with as much goodwill and self-
esteem as possible under the circumstances.

What of the aftermath, the period after the downsizing? It
was something of a shock to the senior managers of this division
when they realized how the survivors felt. In spite of all of their
good intentions and hard work in trying to create a more open
and honest environment using a fair and respectful selection
process, the single most prevalent reaction in the survivors was
concern about their own job security.

It is clear that the transition in the basic employer-employee
contract continues to be anxiety-producing for the survivors. In
spite of the emphasis by senior managers on the fact that the
redesign was a one-time event, most employees in the company
are aware that cost savings are a continual priority for the divi-

sion, along with improved customer service and product innovation. When moving toward an empowering and participatory work environment, a company cannot stop part way through the process. During the downsizing, this division began to engage its employees in ownership of the business, in understanding its problems, and in finding potential solutions. It treated employees more fairly and equitably than ever before. It is now getting more honest feedback and assertiveness from employees than ever before. These responses create the opportunity to develop the kind of ongoing learning and employee involvement that prevent violence from ever occurring and that make for business success.

As for the senior managers themselves, they are beginning to realize that organizational transitions do not occur overnight. They are also discovering that a key part of keeping the implementation of the new business strategy moving is their own ongoing, active participation with the survivors. At the first key meeting of all the division's leadership and managers after the downsizing, the head of the division discovered that the only way to deal with the continuing uncertainty and anxiety among employees was to share more of himself in a personal, realistic manner. He shared that he was concerned about his job, too. He told his audience that difficult times make all careers uncertain. He went on to say that he believed in the business strategy that management had chosen and that, with employees' help, he believed the company could thrive and grow. The survivors are still talking about that speech. It engaged them in their hearts, and it will inspire their best efforts. The executive took the risk of speaking from his heart in a genuine way. He was real, and it touched his employees in a way that will make them more productive for years to come.

Chapter 10
Conclusion

Workplace violence is growing at an alarming rate, in terms of both frequency and severity. No company and no employee is safe any more from the threat of harm posed by workplace violence. Courts and government regulatory agencies are increasingly holding employers, as individuals and as corporations, liable when violence occurs within their organizations. I believe that there is merit in this trend, because there is strong evidence to support the belief that companies using relatively inexpensive tactics can prevent workplace violence.

This book represents one attempt to demonstrate what can be done to make company workplaces safer for all employees. It is important to realize that the occurrence of violence is situational. It is the result of a spiraling escalation of perceived provocations, reactive thoughts and emotions, and attempts to cope with stress. It has to do with the subjective experience by the employee of the situation he is in. Once employers understand how violence comes about, it is easy to see many of the ways that it can be prevented.

Preventing workplace violence is a complex challenge. We have a long way to go in developing the ability to predict accurately who will eventually become violent in the corporate environment. Because violence can arise from so many sources, there are no simple answers. Strangers who kill while committing crimes such as robbery present a very different set of difficulties in prevention from irate customers or disgruntled employees. Estranged spouses who engage in intimidation and violence represent one of the most challenging types of violence faced by our society. When it spills into the workplace, it becomes especially complicated.

Everyone agrees that supervisors and direct managers represent a key first-line defense in any company's battle against violence. By training supervisors and managers in the warning signs of violence and in the effective use of performance review, a company can help ensure that an employee's intimidating behavior, attitudinal problems, or cries for help will be taken seriously and responded to quickly so that they do not escalate into violence. The presence of toxic supervisors, who need to show their power and authority over others or who lack the ability to respond to workers with any compassion and understanding, is a dangerous risk for any company.

Most people agree that all companies should have violence response teams. Such a team must be prepared to evaluate quickly any risk situations and to respond with appropriate measures. Employee assistance counseling, fitness-for-duty evaluations, and involuntary hospitalization may all be appropriate ways to help an employee whose behavior may be escalating into violence. Potentialities should be anticipated and planned for so that when a crisis occurs staff members know how to handle it and have available the resources they need.

Some people are beginning to realize that the kind of behavior that a company tolerates may be related to the occurrence of violence. If harassment and intimidation are tolerated, if mistrust is prevalent, if prejudice and authoritarianism are the rule, the company is not going to have employees stepping forward to voice their concerns or fears about an escalating co-worker. Nor are they going to trust that the company will intervene in the employee's best interest. The fact is that corporate culture plays a key role in the occurrence of workplace violence and in its prevention. Environments in which people are respected and listened and responded to are much less likely to produce violent events than those that treat people as disposable tools. At worksites with positive environments, an employee who is showing symptoms of withdrawal and isolation, paranoia and rage, helplessness and depression, and all of the other cognitive and emotional indicators of overwhelming stress is likely to be recognized and dealt with. If an employee believes that a supervisor has her best interest at heart, a conflict between them is much more likely to be talked out than fought out.

A company's policies can become tools to help shape the corporate environment. Policies can communicate to employees the behaviors and attitudes that are considered acceptable and productive within a business in order to accomplish its goals. Every company is finding competition increasingly more global and therefore more intense. Change is occurring more rapidly. Work is becoming more complex. Competitive advantage will come to those companies that have the right products and strategy and the corporate culture to achieve them. For many companies, teamwork, trust, and honest communication will be essential to the generation of innovation and quality in both production of goods and provision of services. In the new business world, respect, sharing of information, and participatory partnering will increasingly become necessities as the old paternal promise of employer security continues to drop away. The requirements of the new business realities are the good management practices that mitigate against workplace violence.

How a company responds to the challenge and threat of the possibility of violence will probably be a reflection of the style and personality of the company's leaders and its culture. If you are in one of the companies that continues to deny that violence could occur at your factory or your corporate headquarters, my guess is that your leaders are ignoring other important realities, as well. If your company president is coping with the threat of violence by securing the executive offices with guards and electronic devices, chances are good that she has a bunker mentality that is revealing itself to employees and customers in other repressive and controlling efforts, as well.

On the other hand, if your company leaders realize that how employees feel about the worksite, about one another, and about customers are three of the critical elements in getting the job done, they may be able to take constructive actions to make the environment safer and more productive. If they see that their behavior sets the tone and example for the rest of the organization, they will engage employees as shareholders and partners. They will hold employees accountable but give them the information and support they need to take risks and to succeed. With proper inputs, they will make hard business decisions. They will continue to alter the employer-employee relationship, using processes that are respectful, fair, realistic, and participatory and providing the safety net of services and care that helps all employees make it through the changes.

Appendix

Company Self-Assessment Exercise

By completing the following exercise, you can determine how well your company has taken the necessary steps to prevent workplace violence and what work still needs to be done. Simply check yes or no for each of the questions listed below:

	Yes	No
Employee Hiring		
• Do your job descriptions include requirements for interpersonal behavior (including nonviolence) that are job-related?	☐	☐
• Do you do basic screening for appropriate interpersonal behavior in initial interviews and performance reviews?	☐	☐
• Do you find out how applicants resolve conflict and their beliefs about violence?	☐	☐
• Do you do an adequate job checking references with attention to emotional stability?	☐	☐
• Do hiring practices include background checks, with attention to gaps in employment and to police records?	☐	☐

	Yes	No

Supervisory Skill and Attitudes

- Do you offer management training for front-line leadership on how to deal with emotional behavior? ☐ ☐
- Do your supervisors provide for dignity and choices for your workforce? ☐ ☐
- Is there supervisory training in effective performance review and problem identification? ☐ ☐
- Are performance issues confronted in a timely manner? ☐ ☐
- Are performance issues handled fairly, constructively, positively, and with respect? ☐ ☐
- Do supervisors have and know how to assess resources available to them and to employees (e.g., employee assistance programs, consultation about problem employees, drug and alcohol training programs)? ☐ ☐
- Do they use these resources? ☐ ☐

Violence Preparedness and Training

- Are your supervisors and managers trained to recognize the warning signs of potential violence? ☐ ☐
- Are your supervisors and managers trained to deal with performance problems (one of the early signs of possible instability in a worker)? ☐ ☐
- Do you have access to internal and expert resources, including EAP, medical staff, forensic and risk evaluators, and security personnel, in order to do fitness-for-duty and risk assessments? ☐ ☐

	Yes	No
• Do you have a written assessment plan outlining how to deal with threatening situations?	☐	☐
• Do you have a threat management team in place to assess risk in a given situation, to keep the company prepared for crisis management, and to provide ongoing training to managers?	☐	☐
• Is there an effective communication channel in place when a problem or potential problem is identified?	☐	☐

Policies and Procedures

	Yes	No
• Do you have clear policies about intimidation, harassment, threats of violence, violent or destructive behavior, and the use of drugs or alcohol?	☐	☐
• Does your company have clear polices and procedures regarding violence?	☐	☐
• Do your policies regarding problem resolution ensure that the procedures are fair, perceived as fair, and timely?	☐	☐
• Do you have sufficient mental health resources, whether internal or external, to deal with postviolence trauma to employees and to the victim's family?	☐	☐
• Do you have a communication plan for dealing with the media should there be a violent incident?	☐	☐
• Do you offer health promotion and education programs on personal safety, sexual harassment, employee assistance, and stress management?	☐	☐
• Do your policies require a review of the human or personal elements before people are let go or disciplined?	☐	☐

	Yes	No
• Are necessary layoffs or terminations done in a humane manner with adequate support services?	☐	☐
• Do displacement strategies include elements that preserve dignity, including outplacement resources?	☐	☐

Organization Culture

	Yes	No
• Do employees believe that they will be treated fairly and with respect?	☐	☐
• Are there systems of communication that allow employees to air concerns and grievances constructively?	☐	☐
• Do people know one another well enough to know and care if someone is under severe stress?	☐	☐
• Is it socially acceptable to seek help from HR or an EAP?	☐	☐
• Is poor performance dealt with directly, constructively, and quickly rather than ignored or tolerated?	☐	☐
• Does an organizational environment exist in which employees feel fairly treated, respected, allowed to have input? Is communication honest, encouraged, and aboveboard?	☐	☐

Physical Facilities/Environmental Design, Building Security

	Yes	No
• Have you assessed physical security systems?	☐	☐
• Do you have a backup communication system in case phones are damaged or jammed?	☐	☐

	Yes	No
• Can you communicate quickly to large numbers of employees after an incident to reduce anxiety and rumors?	☐	☐
• Is there a system to control public access to work areas?	☐	☐
• Have you limited exposure of employees where possible?	☐	☐
• Is the room where grievance meetings are held secure?	☐	☐
• Are security precautions taken at grievance or other special meetings?	☐	☐
• Do you have panic buttons on desks of particularly vulnerable staff?	☐	☐
• Do you have a system that controls access of former employees to work areas?	☐	☐
• Have you evaluated the amount of employee contact with strangers and customers?	☐	☐
• Do you provide key cards or some form of identification?	☐	☐
• Does your product or service antagonize some groups of people?	☐	☐
• If you use an external security firm: —How much training does the security company offer?	☐	☐
—Do security personnel get out and meet employees, know what is happening, and make themselves visible and approachable?	☐	☐

You have completed the Company Self-Assessment Exercise. To determine how well your company is prepared to prevent violence, go back to each question to which you answered no. These are the areas where you company needs to take further action. Make a list of these items, and develop an action plan to address each of them.

References

Boxall, Bettina, and Frederick M. Muir. "Prosecutors Taking Harder Line Toward Spouse Abuse," *Los Angeles Times* (July 11, 1994).

Brandt, Gerald T., and Joseph M. Brennan. "Workplace Time Bombs Can Be Diffused," *Human Resource Professional* (Summer 1993).

Burke, Thomas P., Esq., and Daniel Weisberg, Esq. (unpublished). "Workplace Violence: Employer Obligations"

Cameron, K.S., et al. "Best Practices in White-Collar Downsizing: Managing Contradictions," *Academy of Management Executive* (August 1991), pp. 57–73.

Cascio, Wayne F. "Downsizing: What Do We Know? What Have We Learned?" *Academy of Management Executive* (February 1993), pp. 95–104.

Irwin, J. "Safe and Sound: Caseworker Safety in the Delivery of Social Services" (New York: Institute for Families and Children).

Kotter, John P., and James L. Heskett. *Corporate Culture and Performance* (New York: Free Press), 1992.

Kübler-Ross, Elisabeth. *On Death and Dying* (New York: Macmillan, 1972).

Kuzmits, F. "When Employees Kill Other Employees: The Case of Joseph T. Wesbecker," *Journal of Occupational Medicine*, 32:10 (October 1990).

"Let the Good Times Roll—And a Few More Heads," *Business Week* (January 31, 1994).

Lidz, C., et al. "The Accuracy of Predictions of Violence to Others," *Journal of American Medical Associations*, 269:8 (February 24, 1993).

Monahan, J. "Dangerous and Violent Behavior," *Journal of Occupational Medicine*, 1:4 (October–December 1986).

———. "Limiting Therapist Exposure to Tarasoff Liability: Guidelines for Risk Containment," *American Psychologist*, 48:3 (March 1993).

———. "Mental Disorder and Violent Behavior: Perceptions and Evidence," *American Psychologist*, 47:4 (April 1992).

———. "Violence in the Workplace," *Journal of Occupational Medicine*, 32:10 (October 1990).

"Nonviolent Crisis Intervention," National Crisis Prevention Institute, Inc., Brookfield, Wisconsin.

Northwestern National Life Insurance Institute for Occupational Safety and Health survey (1993).

Parks, Paula Lynn. "Guidance on Giving Counsel," *Los Angeles Times* (July 11, 1994).

Platte, Mark. "Witnesses Tell of Shooting at Convair Plant," *Los Angeles Times* (March 14, 1992).

Raimy. "Dodging the Bullet," *HR Executive* (April 1993).

Smith, Bob. "Cease Fire! Preventing Workplace Violence," *HR Focus* (February 1994).

Thurnburg, Linda. "When Violence Hits Business," *HRMagazine* (July 1993).

Index